& ARMS AND THE MAN

NOTES

including
- *Life of the Author*
- *Source of* Pygmalion's *Title*
- *Preface to Each Play*
- *Brief Plot Summary of Each Play*
- *Critical Summaries and Commentaries*
- *List of Characters in Each Play*
- *Character Analyses*
- *Questions for Review*
- *Selected Bibliography*

by
Marilynn O. Harper, M.F.A.
University of Oklahoma

INCORPORATED

LINCOLN, NEBRASKA   68501

Editor

Gary Carey, M.A.
University of Colorado

Consulting Editor

James L. Roberts, Ph.D.
Department of English
University of Nebraska

ISBN 0-8220-1103-4
© Copyright 1981
by
C. K. Hillegass
All Rights Reserved
Printed in U.S.A.

1990 Printing

Cliffs Notes, Inc.   Lincoln, Nebraska

CONTENTS

PYGMALION

ARMS AND THE MAN

LIFE OF THE AUTHOR

It is with good reason that Archibald Henderson, official biographer of his subject, entitled his work *George Bernard Shaw: Man of the Century*. Well before his death at the age of ninety-four, this famous dramatist and critic had become an institution. Among the literate, no set of initials were more widely known than G.B.S. Born on July 26, 1856, in Dublin, Ireland, Shaw survived until November 2, 1950. His ninetieth birthday in 1946 was the occasion for an international celebration, the grand old man being presented with a *festschrift* entitled *GBS 90* to which many distinguished writers contributed. A London publishing firm bought space in the *Times* to voice its greetings:

GBS

Hail to thee, blithe spirit!

Shaw was the third child and only son in a family which he once described as "shabby but genteel." His father, George Carr Shaw, was employed as a civil servant and later became a not too successful merchant. Shaw remembered especially his father's "alcoholic antics"; the old man was a remorseful, yet an unregenerate drinker. It was from his father that Shaw inherited his superb comic gift. Lucinda Gurley Shaw, the mother, was a gifted singer and music teacher; she led her son to develop a passion for music, particularly operatic music. At an early age he had memorized, among others, the works of Mozart, whose fine workmanship he never ceased to admire. Somewhat later, he taught himself to play the piano—in the Shavian manner.

One of the maxims in *The Revolutionist's Handbook*, appended to *Man and Superman*, reads: "He who can does. He who can't teaches." Shaw, who was to insist that all art should be didactic, viewed himself as a kind of teacher, yet he himself had little respect for schoolmasters and formal education. First, his uncle, the Reverend

George Carroll, tutored him. Then at the age of ten, he became a pupil at Wesleyan Connexional School in Dublin and later attended two other schools for short periods of time. He hated them all and declared that he had learned absolutely nothing. But Shaw possessed certain qualities which are not always developed in the classroom—for example, an inquisitive mind and a boundless capacity for independent study. Once asked about his early education, he replied: "I can remember no time at which a page of print was not intelligible to me and can only suppose I was born literate." He went on to add that by the age of ten he had saturated himself in the works of Shakespeare and also in the Bible.

A depleted family exchequer led Shaw to accept employment as a clerk in a Land Agency when he was sixteen. He was unhappy and, determined to become a professional writer, he resigned after five years of service and joined his mother, who was then teaching music in London. The year was 1876. During the next three years he allowed his mother to support him, and he concentrated largely on trying to support himself as an author. No less than five novels came from his pen between the years 1879 and 1883, but it was soon evident that Shaw's genius would never be revealed as a novelist.

In 1879, Shaw was induced to accept employment in a firm promoting the new Edison telephone, his duties being those of a right-of-way agent. He detested the task of interviewing residents in the East End of London and endeavoring to get their permission for the installation of telephone poles and equipment. A few months of such work was enough for him. In his own words, this was the last time he "sinned against his nature" by seeking to earn an honest living.

The year 1879 had greater significance for Shaw. He joined the Zetetical Society, a debating club, the members of which held lengthy discussions on such subjects as economics, science, and religion. Soon he found himself in demand as a speaker and a regular participant at public meetings. At one such meeting held in September, 1882, he listened spellbound to Henry George, an apostle of Land Nationalization and the Single Tax. Shaw credits the American lecturer and author with having roused his interest in economics and social theory; previously, he had concerned himself chiefly with the conflict between science and religion. When Shaw was told that no one could do justice to George's theories without being familiar with the theories of Karl Marx, Shaw promptly read a

French translation of *Das Kapital*, no English translation being then available. He was immediately converted to socialism.

The year 1884 is also a notable one in the life of Bernard Shaw (as he preferred to be called). After reading a tract entitled *Why Are the Many Poor?* and learning that it was published by the Fabian Society, he appeared at the society's next meeting. The intellectual temper of this group, which included such distinguished men as Havelock Ellis, immediately attracted him. He was accepted as a member on September 5 and was elected to the Executive Committee in January. Among the debaters at the Zetetical Society was Sidney Webb, a man whom Shaw recognized as his "natural complement." He easily persuaded Webb to become a Fabian. The two, along with the gifted Mrs. Webb, became the pillars of the society which preached the gospel of constitutional and evolutionary social ism. Shaw's views, voiced in public parks and meeting halls, are expounded at length in *The Intelligent Woman's Guide to Socialism and Capitalism* (1928); many of his ideas also find a place in his dramas.

In the next stage of his career, Shaw emerged as a literary, music, and art critic. Largely because of the influence of William Archer, the distinguished dramatic critic now best remembered as the editor and translator of Ibsen, Shaw became a member of the reviewing staff of the *Pall Mall Gazette* in 1885. Earlier, he had ghostwritten some music reviews for G. L. Lee, with whom his mother had long been associated as a singer and as a music teacher. But this new assignment provided him with his first real experience as a critic. Not long thereafter, and again through the assistance of William Archer, Shaw added to these duties those of an art critic on the widely influential *World*. Archer insisted that Shaw knew very little about art but realised that Shaw *thought* that he did—which was what mattered. As for Shaw, he blandly explained that the way to learn about art was to look at pictures; he had begun doing so years earlier in the Dublin National Gallery.

Shaw's close association with William Archer was paramount in his championing the dramas of Henrik Ibsen as a new, highly original dramatist whose works represented a complete break with the popular theater of the day. "When Ibsen came from Norway," Shaw was to write, "with his characters who thought and discussed as well as acted, the theatrical heaven rolled up like a scroll." Whereas the general public, nurtured on "well-made" romantic and melodramatic plays, denounced Ibsen as a "muck-ferreting dog," Shaw recognized that Ibsen was a great ethical philosopher and a social critic – a role which recommended itself to Shaw himself. On July 18, 1890, Shaw read a paper on Ibsen at a meeting of the Fabian Society. Amplified, this became *The Quintessence of Ibsen* (1891). Sometimes called *The Quintessence of Shaw*, it sets forth the author's profoundest views on the function of the dramatist, who, Shaw believed, should concern himself foremost with how his characters react to various social forces and who should concern himself further with a new morality based upon an examination and challenge of conventional mores.

In view of what Shaw had written about Ibsen (and about himself) and because of Shaw's dedicated activities as a socialist exhorter, *The Widowers' Houses*, his first play, may be called characteristic. Structurally, it represents no departure from the tradition of the well-made play; that is, the action is plotted so that the key situation is exposed in the second act, and the third act is devoted to its resolution. But thematically, the play was revolutionary in England. It dealt with the evils of slum-landlordism, a subject hardly calculated to regale the typical Victorian audience. Produced at J. T. Grein's Independent Theatre in London, it became a sensation because of its "daring" theme, but it was never a theatrical success. Shaw, however, was not at all discouraged. The furor delighted him. No one knew better than he the value of attracting attention. He was already at work on *The Philanderer*, an amusing but rather slight comedy of manners.

In 1894, Shaw's *Arms and the Man* enjoyed a good run at the Avenue Theatre from April 21 to July 7, and it has been revived from time to time to this very day. At last, the real Shaw had emerged – the dramatist who united irrepressible gaiety and complete seriousness of purpose. The play has been described as "a satire on the prevailing bravura style," and it sets forth the "view of romance as the great heresy to be swept from art and life."

In the same year, Shaw wrote *Mrs. Warren's Profession*, which became a *cause célèbre*. Shaw himself grouped it with his so-called "Unpleasant Plays." Dealing with the economic causes of prostitution and the conflict between the prostitute mother and her daughter, it created a tumult which was kept alive for several years on both sides of the Atlantic. It may well be argued that in this play

Shaw was far more the polemist than the artist, but the play still has its place among the provocative dramas of ideas.

The indefatigable Shaw was already at work on his first unquestionably superior play, *Candida*. First produced in 1895, it has been popular ever since and has found its place in anthologies. Notable for effective character portrayal and the adroit use of inversions, it tells how Candida and the Reverend Morrell, widely in public demand as an advanced thinker, reached an honest and sound basis for a lasting marriage.

While working with the Fabians, Shaw met the personable Charlotte Payne-Townshend, an Irish heiress deeply concerned with the many problems of social justice. He was immediately attracted to her. After she had helped him through a long illness, the two were married in 1898, and she became his modest but capable critic and assistant throughout the years of their marriage.

During this period there was no surcease of playwriting on Shaw's part. He completed *You Never Can Tell, The Man of Destiny*, and *The Devil's Disciple*. This last play, an inverted Victorian-type melodrama first acted in the United States, was an immediate success, financially and otherwise. By the turn of the century, Shaw had written *Caesar and Cleopatra* and *The Admirable Bashville*. He was now the acknowledged major force in the new drama of the twentieth century.

The year 1903 is especially memorable for the completion and publication of *Man and Superman*. It was first acted (without the Don Juan in Hell intermezzo which constitutes Act III) in 1905. Then, some twenty-three other plays were added to the Shavian canon as the century advanced toward the halfway mark. Best known among these are *Major Barbara* (1905), *Androcles and the Lion* (1912), *Pygmalion* (1912), *Heartbreak House* (1916), *Back to Methuselah* (1921), and *Saint Joan* (1923). During the years 1930-32, the Ayot St. Lawrence Edition of his collected plays was published. Shaw's literary pre-eminence had found world-wide recognition. He refused, however, to accept either a knighthood or the Order of Merit offered by the Crown, but in 1926 he did accept the Nobel Prize for Literature. It was quite typical of him to state that the award was given to him by a grateful public because he had not published anything during that year.

Shaw persistently rejected offers from film makers. According to one story, when importuned by Samuel Goldwyn, the well-known Hollywood producer, he replied: "The difficulty, Mr. Goldwyn, is that you are an artist and I am a business man." Later, however, the ardor and ability of Gabriel Pascal impressed him, and he agreed to prepare the scenario of *Pygmalion* for production. The film, released in 1938, was a notable success. *Major Barbara* and *Androcles and the Lion* followed, and the Irish-born dramatist had now won a much larger audience. *My Fair Lady*, a musical adapted from *Pygmalion*, opened in New Haven, Connecticut, on February 4, 1956, starring Rex Harrison and Julie Andrews, and it was and remains a spectacular success. A film version won an Academy Award in 1964 as Best Picture.

Discussing *Macbeth*, Shaw once wrote: "I want to be thoroughly used up when I die, for the harder I work, the more I live. I rejoice in life for its own sake. Life is no 'brief candle' for me. It is a sort of splendid torch, which I have got hold of for the moment; and I want to make it burn as brightly as possible before handing it on to future generations." Life indeed was a bright torch which burned long for Bernard Shaw. Almost to the very end, when he was bedridden with a broken hip, he lived up to his credo. He was ninety-two years old in 1949, when *Buoyant Billions* was produced at the Malvern Festival. In the same year his highly readable *Sixteen Self Sketches* was published. He was planning the writing of still another play when he died on November 2, 1950.

THE SOURCE OF THE TITLE: THE LEGEND OF PYGMALION AND GALATEA

Shaw took his title from the ancient Greek legend of the famous sculptor named Pygmalion who could find nothing good in women, and, as a result, he resolved to live out his life unmarried. However, he carved a statue out of ivory that was so beautiful and so perfect that he fell in love with his own creation. Indeed, the statue was so perfect that no living being could possibly be its equal. Consequently, at a festival, he prayed to the goddess of love, Aphrodite, that he might have the statue come to life. When he reached home, to his amazement, he found that his wish had been fulfilled, and he proceeded to marry the statue, which he named Galatea.

Even though Shaw used several aspects of the legend, most prominently one of the names in the title, viewers, writers, critics, and audiences have consistently insisted upon there being some truth attached to every analogy in the myth. First of all, in Shaw's *Pygmalion*, Professor Henry Higgins is the most renowned man of phonetics of his time; Higgins is also like Pygmalion in his view of women—cynical and derogatory: Higgins says, "I find that the moment I let a woman make friends with me, she becomes jealous, exacting, suspicious, and a damned nuisance." And whereas in the myth, Pygmalion carved something beautiful out of raw stone and gave it life, Shaw's Higgins takes a "guttersnipe," a "squashed cabbage leaf" up out of the slums and makes her into an exquisite work of art. Here, however, the analogies end. Shaw's "Galatea," Eliza, develops a soul of her own and a fierce independence from her creator.

In the popular film version and in the even more popular musical comedy version (*My Fair Lady*), the ending allows the audience to see a romantic love interest that blends in with the ancient myth. This, however, is a sentimentalized version of Shaw's play. Shaw provided no such tender affection to blossom between professor and pupil.

PREFACE TO PYGMALION

Shaw ultimately wrote a preface to almost all of his plays that he considered important. In fact, sometimes the Prefaces, the Prologues, and the Afterwords exceeded the length of the original dramas. In one of his prefaces, he comments that most dramatists use the preface to expound on things that have little or no importance to the drama. Here, Shaw's preface does not comment upon the drama that is to follow, but instead, since the play deals with phonetics, and since the character of Henry Higgins is based largely upon a man named Henry Sweet, and since Shaw ultimately *did* leave a large sum of money upon his death for a thorough revision of English spelling rules, he uses this preface to comment upon the absurdity of English spelling in connection with English pronunciation. Finally, Shaw sarcastically refers to those critics who say that a successful play should never be didactic; this play is obviously didactic, and it has been immensely popular ever since it was first presented.

BRIEF PLOT SUMMARY

On a summer evening in London's Covent Garden, a group of assorted people are gathered together under the portico of St. Paul's Church for protection from the rain. Among the group are Mrs. Eynsford-Hill and her daughter, Clara, who are waiting for the son, Freddy, to return with a cab. When he returns in failure, he is again sent in search of a cab. As he leaves, he collides with a young flower girl with a thick Cockney accent, and he ruins many of her flowers. After he is gone, the mother is interested in how such a "low" creature could know her son's name; she discovers that the flower girl calls everyone either "Freddy" or "Charlie." When an elderly gentleman comes into the shelter, the flower girl notes his distinguished appearance and tries to coax him to buy some flowers. This gentleman, Colonel Pickering, refuses to buy the flowers, but he gives the girl some money. Members of the crowd warn the girl against taking the money because there is a man behind her taking notes of everything she says. When the flower girl (Eliza) loudly proclaims that "I am a good girl, I am," the bystanders begin to protest. The note taker, it turns out, is Professor Henry Higgins, an expert in phonetics. His hobby is identifying everyone's accent and place of birth. He even maintains that he could take this "ragamuffin" of a flower girl and teach her to talk like a duchess in three months. At this time, the elder gentleman identifies himself as Colonel Pickering, the author of a book on Sanskrit, who has come to meet the famous Henry Higgins, to whom he is now talking. The two go off to discuss their mutual interest in phonetics.

The next morning at Professor Higgins' house, the two men are discussing Higgins' experiments when the flower girl is announced by Mrs. Pearce, Higgins' housekeeper. The girl, Eliza Doolittle, remembers that Higgins bragged about being able to teach her to speak like a duchess, and she has come to take lessons so that she can get a position in a flower shop. Pickering makes a wager with Higgins, who, in the spirit of good sport, decides to take the bet: he orders Mrs. Pearce to take the girl away, scrub her, and burn her clothes. He overcomes all of Eliza's objections, and Eliza is taken away. At this time, Eliza's father appears with the intention of blackmailing Higgins, but he is so intimidated by Higgins that he ends up asking for five pounds because he is one of the "*un*deserving poor." Higgins is so pleased with the old fellow's audacity and his unique view of morality that he gives him the five pounds and is immediately rid of him.

Sometime later, Higgins brings Eliza to his mother's house during her "receiving day." Freddy Eynsford-Hill and his mother and sister Clara are also present. These turn out to be the same people whom we saw under the portico in the first act. Now, however, none of the guests recognize that Eliza is the "ragamuffin" flower girl of that night. Everyone is amused with the pedantic correctness of her speech and are even more impressed with Eliza's narration of her aunt's death, told in perfect English, but told with lurid and shocking details. After Eliza's departure, Mrs. Higgins points out that the girl is far from being ready to be presented in public.

Some time later, Higgins, Pickering, and Eliza return late in the evening. The men are delighted with the great success they have had that day in passing off Eliza as a great duchess at an ambassador's garden party. They are so extremely proud that they totally ignore Eliza and her contribution to the success of the "experiment." Infuriated, Eliza finally throws a slipper at Higgins, only to be informed that she is being unreasonable. Eliza is concerned with what will happen to her now that the experiment is over: is she to be tossed back into the gutter; what is her future place? Higgins cannot see that this is a problem, and after telling her that all of the clothes that she has been wearing belong to her, he retires for the evening.

The next day, Higgins arrives at his mother's house completely baffled that Eliza has disappeared. He has telephoned the police and is then surprised to learn that Eliza is upstairs. While waiting for Eliza, Mr. Doolittle enters and he accuses Higgins of ruining him because Higgins told a wealthy man that Doolittle was England's most original moralist, and, as a result, the man left an enormous sum of money in trust for Doolittle to lecture on moral reforms. He has thus been forced into middle-class morality, and he and his common-law wife are miserable. He has come to invite Eliza to his wedding, another concession to dreadful middle-class morality.

Eliza enters and agrees to come to her father's wedding. As they all prepare to leave, Higgins restrains Eliza and tries to get her to return to his house. He maintains that he treats everyone with complete equality. To him, he makes no social distinction between the way he would treat a flower girl or a duchess. Eliza is determined to have respect and independence, and thus she refuses to return to Higgins' house. Higgins then admits that he misses her and also admires her newfound independence. He further maintains that she should return, and the three of them will live equally, as "three bachelors." Eliza, however, feels otherwise, and she leaves with Mrs. Higgins to attend her father's wedding.

LIST OF CHARACTERS

Professor Henry Higgins

Higgins is a forty-year-old bachelor who specializes in phonetics and who is an acclaimed authority on the subject of dialects, accents, and phonetics.

Eliza Doolittle

She is an uneducated, uncouth "guttersnipe," the flower girl whom Higgins (for a dare) decides to mold into a duchess. She is probably twenty years younger than Higgins.

Alfred Doolittle

Eliza's father; he is a dustman with a sonorous voice and a Welsh accent, who proudly believes in his position as a member of the "undeserving poor."

Colonel Pickering

A distinguished retired officer and the author of *Spoken Sanskrit*. He has come to England to meet the famous Professor Henry Higgins. He is courteous and polite to Eliza, and he shares in Higgins' experiments in phonetics in teaching Eliza to speak as a duchess.

Mrs. Higgins

Henry Higgins' mother, who thoroughly loves her son but also thoroughly disapproves of his manners, his language, and his social behavior.

Mrs. Eynsford-Hill

A lady of the upper-middle class who is in a rather impoverished condition but is still clinging to her gentility.

Clara Eynsford-Hill

Her daughter; she tries to act the role of the modern, advanced young person.

Freddy Eynsford-Hill

Her son; he is a pleasant young man who is enchanted by Eliza upon first meeting her.

Mrs. Pearce

Professor Higgins' housekeeper of long standing. She is the one who first sees the difficulty of what is to happen to Eliza after Higgins and Pickering have finished their experiment with her.

SUMMARIES AND COMMENTARIES

ACT I

Summary

Act I opens in Covent Garden under the portico of St. Paul's Church during a heavy summer rain immediately after a theatrical performance has let out. All types and levels of society are huddled here to avoid the rain. Mrs. Eynsford-Hill is complaining to her daughter Clara that her son Freddy has been gone an intolerably long time in search of a cab. When he suddenly returns with the announcement that there is not a cab to be had for love nor money, they reprimand him for not trying other places and quickly send him off to try again in another direction.

As Freddy reopens his umbrella and dashes off, he accidentally collides with a flower girl, who is hurrying for shelter, and knocks over her basket of flowers. In a heavy, almost incomprehensible,

Cockney accent, she familiarly calls him by his name (Freddy) and tells him to watch where he is going. She then sits and begins to rearrange her flowers, mumbling to herself about the carelessness of such people who knock others about.

Mrs. Eynsford-Hill, who has heard the entire episode, is consumed with curiosity as to how this low-class, badly dressed ragamuffin with such a dreadful accent could possibly know her son well enough to call him by his first name. The flower girl (Liza or Eliza) asks, first, if the lady will pay for the flowers that Freddy just ruined, and against Clara's objections, Mrs. Eynsford-Hill pays the girl generously and then learns that Eliza merely calls all strangers either Freddy or Charlie.

At this moment, "an elderly gentleman of the amiable military type" rushes in for shelter. Eliza immediately tries to sell him some flowers, but he refuses because he has nothing smaller than a "sovereign." Eliza badgers him by insisting that she can change a large coin. Suddenly, a bystander warns the flower girl to be careful because there is a stranger who is taking down everything she says. Frightened that she might be accused of soliciting for immoral purposes, Eliza loudly maintains her right to sell flowers "if I keep off the kerb." Her loud and continual protestation attracts everyone's attention until finally the notetaker (Professor Henry Higgins) tells her to "shut up." He resents the fact that she mistakes him for a policeman or a spy for the police. Eliza wants to see what he has written, and when she can't read the "shorthand," he reads off what he has written. It is an exact Cockney phonetic rendition of her own speech patterns.

At this point, the elderly gentleman (Colonel Pickering) and others take the girl's side, and as the group begins to talk to the notetaker, he (Professor Higgins) begins to identify where each of the speakers was born and where they live. He can even identify their locality inside the city of London. When Mrs. Eynsford-Hill complains about the weather, the notetaker (Higgins) points out that the rain has stopped, and everyone disperses except the gentleman (Colonel Pickering) and the flower girl (Eliza).

When the gentleman inquires about the notetaker's talents, he discloses that he is a student of phonetics; in fact, his profession is teaching wealthy people who aspire to climb the social ladder to speak properly. While he explains his profession, Eliza continually makes unutterable, horrible sounds, even though Higgins constantly tells her to cease making these "detestable" noises; he then brags that "in three months I could pass that girl off as a duchess at an ambassador's garden party." (In the next act, the time is "six months, three if she has a good ear.")

When the elderly gentleman identifies himself as a "student of Indian dialects," by the name of Colonel Pickering, author of *Spoken Sanskrit*, Higgins then introduces himself as Henry Higgins, author of Higgins' *Universal Alphabet*. It turns out that Pickering came to England to meet Higgins, and that Higgins was about to embark on a journey to India to meet Pickering. As they are about to leave together to discuss their mutual interests, Eliza interrupts with a plea for money saying, "I'm short for my lodging." Higgins reminds her she is lying because she had previously said that she could change a half-a-crown; nevertheless, he throws her a mess of coins which she excitedly scoops up, accompanied by all sorts of unintelligible Cockney sounds.

At this point, Freddy Eynsford-Hill returns with a cab, but doesn't know what to do with it since everyone has left. Eliza, thanks to the sudden windfall of money from Higgins, engages the cab to take her home, leaving Freddy alone and perplexed.

Commentary

Pygmalion is perhaps Shaw's most famous play and, ironically, it is among his most abused and misinterpreted ones. Almost everyone knows the basic outlines of this story of the Cockney flower girl who is almost magically transformed into a duchess by taking speech (phonetic) lessons from her famous professor. The abuse comes partly from the fact that Shaw subtitled his play, "A Romance." In the popular adaptations (the film of 1938 and the musical *My Fair Lady*), "romance" was written into the script and inserted into the relationship between Higgins and Eliza — in fact, the title of the play, *Pygmalion*, being based on the legend of a person who fell in love with his creation, could easily give rise to this wrong interpretation. In fact, one advertisement claims that the play is one of the most "beautiful love stories" that the world has ever read. Yet, as noted elsewhere, Shaw used the term "romance" in its more restricted form, meaning the implausibility of actually transforming a flower girl into a grand duchess by the simple means of using phonetic instruction. Yet, in spite of Shaw's own pronouncements and in spite of all the evidence in the play, readers and audiences still continue to sentimentalize over the outcome of the play and refuse to recognize the anti-romantic aspect of the drama.

The opening scene of the drama captures many of the diverse elements running throughout the play. Brought together by the common necessity of protection from a sudden downpour, we encounter such diverse types as the impoverished middle-class Eynsford-Hills, with their genteel pretensions and disdain, a wealthy Anglo-Indian gentleman (Colonel Pickering), who seems quite tolerant, a haughty egotistical professor (Higgins), who seems exceptionally intolerant, an indistinct group of nondescript bystanders, and also a pushy, rude flower girl who embodies the essence of vulgarity. These diverse characters would never be found together except by the necessity of something like a sudden rain shower. This serves Shaw dramatically because he needs a variety of accents so that Professor Higgins can demonstrate his brilliance at identifying dialects and places of birth, according to his science of phonetics. Note also that his performance arouses both antagonism and appreciation in the crowd. The antagonism is based upon the fact that the crowd, at first, believes that he is a spy for the police, and second, even after identifying where they come from, he is intruding upon some private aspect of their lives which they might want to cover up—that is, due to false pride or snobbism, many people want to disguise the place of their birth; thus, Professor Higgins, they think, in identifying the backgrounds of some of the members of the crowd is also revealing something about their pasts. Ironically, Professor Higgins' occupation is teaching wealthy people how to speak properly so that they can *conceal* their backgrounds. In the next act, Eliza will come to him so that her own origins can be concealed from the public.

Shaw is also dramatically exhibiting two types of vulgarity here. first, the vulgarity of the lower class, as seen in Eliza, and second, the "refined" vulgarity of the middle class as seen in Clara Eynsford-Hill. We should remember that one of the aims of the play is an attack (through the character of Alfred Doolittle) on middle-class morality and restrictions. Eliza's vulgarity is a result of necessity, forcing her to wheedle a few coins from bystanders; it is both comic and pathetic. Her vulgarity is comic as she tries to cozen money out of the bystanders, and it is vulgarly pathetic when she is suspected of soliciting as a prostitute. Unjustly, Eliza can be falsely accused of prostitution because she belongs to a class of society where prostitution is an assumed practice, and she can also be pigeonholed in a class of society which cannot afford a lawyer for protection. Consequently, Eliza can only prove her innocence of such a charge by loudly proclaiming to everyone "I'm a good girl, I am." Ultimately, the most vulgar thing about Eliza is her disgusting and animalistic use of the English language, a habit that elicits the wrath of Professor Higgins and thus sets up the dramatic premise for the rest of the drama.

In contrast to Eliza, Clara Eynsford-Hill would superficially seem to be without a trace of vulgarity. But she represents aspects of the middle class which Shaw and Doolittle reject – that is, Clara is pushy, unfriendly, and disdainful of people whom she considers beneath her, and she is offended unnecessarily by strangers (such as Higgins) who speak to her (notice her hypocricy later in Act III when she meets Higgins socially and is sycophantly obeisant to him). Ironically, in the next act, Eliza will want to become very much like Clara and will come to Higgins to take lessons for that purpose.

It is Higgins who ultimately occupies center stage. At first, he is only the bystander at the edge of the crowd. Then he slowly takes charge because of his talent, his wit, and his domineering character. In a play that will focus a great deal on the varying concepts of manners, Higgins is first noted for his *lack* of manners. On first sight, he is as rude in his outspokenness, as Eliza is crude in her pronunciation. He seems to take pleasure in bullying other people, especially people who are socially beneath him, even though he maintains that he is *not* a snob. He can spurt out a tirade of venom when he hears the English language so completely and disgustingly vilified, and he directs his venom directly at Eliza:

> A woman who utters such depressing and disgusting sounds has no right to be anywhere – no right to live. Remember that you are a human being with a soul and the divine gift of articulate speech: that your native language is the language of Shakespeare and Milton and the Bible; and

don't sit there crooning like a bilious pigeon. [We have stan-
dardized Shaw's unique grammar and spelling.]

Whether or not Higgins is right in his appraisal is not the point here;
even though he is amusingly right, a man who would publicly utter
such derogatory comments about another human being for the purpose of showing off in front of a crowd of people is certainly no
gentleman. To the contrary, he is another type of vulgarian; he is a
person without consideration for the feelings of others, one who is
totally lacking in social manners, and his absence of manners will
become the subject of Mrs. Pearce's concern in the next act, when
Higgins decides to take Eliza into his house.

After the above speech, Higgins boastfully announces to the
gathered crowd that "in three months I could pass that girl off as a
duchess at an ambassador's garden party." Consequently, this sentence provides the impetus for the remainder of the play, and it will
evoke the larger questions of the drama – that is, do speech patterns
determine the quality of a person's manners and nature? Higgins
will be able to teach her to pronounce words as a duchess would, but
how important are phonetics in determining the true nature of a person's worth? Thus, as noted in the preface, Shaw somewhat misled
the reader when he suggested that the play was about phonetics. Instead, Shaw is using phonetics only as a basis for a comment on
manners in general. And Shaw's final comment on manners involves
the comic display of manners as Eliza affects the manners of a *grand
dame* in engaging the cab to take her home.

ACT II

Summary

The scene shifts to Higgins' laboratory in his home in Wimpole
Street. It is eleven o'clock the next morning, and Higgins has been
giving Pickering some demonstrations of the types of equipment
that he uses in recording sounds which can then be studied at leisure
in a scientific manner. As Higgins finishes his demonstration,
Pickering admits that he is impressed, but he hasn't been able to
follow more than half of what Higgins has shown him. Mrs. Pearce,
the housekeeper, enters to announce that there is a strange girl,
"quite a common girl," downstairs asking for the professor. Higgins

is puzzled, but he thinks that this would be a good opportunity to record her in Pickering's presence, particularly since she is reported to have an unusual accent. He will thus be able to show Pickering how he makes records, using various pieces of his equipment that he has been demonstrating.

Eliza, the flower girl from the preceding evening, enters. She is now dressed in an outlandish outfit, consisting of, among other things, three ostrich feathers of orange, sky-blue, and red. When Higgins recognizes her, he orders her away because he has already recorded enough of her type of "Lisson Grove lingo." Eliza, however, has come in a taxi, with a proposition. Higgins is not impressed and rudely inquires: "Shall we ask this baggage to sit down, or shall we throw her out of the window?" Pickering is more solicitous, and so Eliza turns to him and reveals that she wants to obtain a job as a lady in a flower shop, but she won't be hired unless she can speak in a genteel, ladylike fashion; thus, she has come to take speech lessons from Higgins because last night, he bragged about his ability to teach proper speech to anyone. She is even willing to pay as much as a shilling an hour (about twenty-five cents an hour, an absurdly ridiculous sum – so absurdly low, in fact, that it appeals to Higgins' imagination). Higgins calculates that Eliza's offer is a certain proportion of her daily income, and therefore represents, for her, a large payment. While he is considering the arrangement, Pickering, whose interest has also been aroused, makes a wager: "I'll bet you all the expenses of the experiment," he tells Higgins, that the professor cannot teach Eliza to speak "like a duchess" in six months' time and pass her off at an ambassador's garden party as a "lady." Furthermore, Pickering says, ironically, "And I'll pay for the lessons," since the lessons are only twenty-five cents an hour. Higgins is indeed tempted – the challenge is tremendously great because Eliza is "so deliciously low – so horribly dirty –." Thus he decides to do it: he "shall make a duchess of this draggletailed guttersnipe" in "six months – in three if she has a good ear and a quick tongue." He then orders Mrs. Pearce to take her away, to scrub her down, to burn her clothes and to get her new ones. And if she makes any noise, he says, Mrs. Pearce should "wallop her."

Both Eliza and Mrs. Pearce are horrified over these suggestions. Mrs. Pearce suggests that perhaps the girl is married or that perhaps she might have parents who would object. But, as it turns out, Eliza's parents turned her out to earn her own living over two years ago. Once again, Higgins bullies the girl, ordering her about and ignoring her feelings to the point that Pickering reminds him that Eliza "has some feelings," but Higgins ignores the possibility and concentrates on the immediate problem with Eliza: it is not the pronunciation; it is the grammar that will be the problem.

Mrs. Pearce, before leaving, wonders what is to become of Eliza when they have finished with her. Higgins' response is a vague question about what will become of her if he leaves her alone; to him it makes no difference—when they are through, "we can throw her back into the gutter, and then it will be her own business again." When Eliza begins to revolt, Higgins tempts her with some chocolates and with the thought of some young man wanting to marry her. Eliza relents, and Mrs. Pearce takes her away to be washed.

Following up on Mrs. Pearce's suggestions, Pickering suddenly becomes interested in the morality of their adventure. He questions if Higgins is "a man of good character where women are concerned?" Higgins admits that he has never known how to deal with women, because the moment you "let a woman into your life," she becomes "jealous, exacting, suspicious and a damned nuisance." Furthermore, he says, the moment *he* becomes friends with a woman, *he* becomes "selfish and tyrannical." Thus, he is "a confirmed old bachelor" and plans to remain one, and he assures Pickering that he will not take advantage of Eliza.

Mrs. Pearce returns with Eliza's hat which Eliza wants saved, and she asks Higgins to watch his behavior around the young girl— that is, he should try to cease swearing, use better table manners and try to act more like a gentleman. Mrs. Pearce then answers the doorbell and informs Higgins that a dustman, Alfred Doolittle, is outside and that he maintains that Higgins has his daughter inside. Pickering warns Higgins that this might be a trap, that Doolittle might be a scoundrel. Higgins is not perturbed and has the man sent for.

Doolittle is an elderly but vigorous man with a remarkably expressive voice. To the contrary of all expectations, there is no dissension because when Doolittle announces that he wants his daughter, Higgins agrees thoroughly; he tells Doolittle to "take her away at once." This both shocks and surprises Doolittle, who definitely does *not* want his daughter; after all, he has taken the trouble once to get rid of her, and he certainly doesn't want her back now.

When Higgins maintains that it is "a plant—a plot to extort money by threats," Doolittle retracts. He maintains that he hasn't seen the girl for two months. As Doolittle talks, Higgins is captivated by the old man's Welsh accent and also by his "mendacity and dishonesty." Doolittle clearly does not want his daughter back; all he wants is a five-pound note in order to go out with his common-law wife and get drunk. When Pickering asks Doolittle if he has no morals, Doolittle quite honestly answers that he can't afford morals, and, further-more, "What's a five-pound note to you? And what's Eliza to me?" Higgins is delighted with Doolittle's cynical view of middle-class morality as Doolittle proclaims himself to be a member of the "un-deserving poor"; there has been too much attention paid to the de-serving poor, he says, and it is time for the likes of him, who arc undeserving, to reap some of the benefits of money. "Undeserving Poverty" is his motto, and if Higgins and Pickering give him five pounds, he promises that he will not save it; by Monday, he will have spent the entire five pounds on one single drunken spree with his "missus." Higgins finds the idea *and* the person irresistible; in fact, he considers giving the man ten pounds, but Doolittle demurs, saying that ten pounds might cause him to feel prudent, whereas five pounds is just enough for a spree. Delighted, Higgins hands Doolittle five pounds and, at that moment, Eliza enters, dressed in a new Japanese kimono. Her father doesn't recognize her at first and is genuinely surprised that she could ever get herself cleaned up to look as good as she does. Eliza immediately warns them all that her father has come for no other purpose than to wheedle money out of them in order to get drunk. Eliza is willing to drop her relations with her father and also to lord it over her old friends, but Higgins warns her not to drop her old friends too quickly. New clothes arrive then for Eliza, and she utters one of those unspeakable noises as she rushes out to see the new clothes: "Ah-ow-oo-ooh!" Both Higgins and Pickering acknowledge that they have indeed taken on a "stiff job."

Commentary

Whereas the first act gave us only a cursory view of Higgins, this act begins to round out many aspects of his personality. Shaw calls him the energetic type who is "violently interested in everything that can be studied as a scientific subject." Consequently, this clue in the printed discussion of his character should warn the reader that Higgins' relationship with Eliza will be based upon *scientific experiments* and that the human element will *not* be foremost in his mind. Likewise, Shaw tells the reader that Higgins fluctuates from genial bullying and good humor to a stormy petulance when things go wrong. Above all, Higgins is totally frank and devoid of any artifice or malice. On the stage, however, Shaw has to present these character concepts to the audience. He does this by having Mrs. Pearce, who has been Higgins' housekeeper for a long time, constantly speak about his character and his habits. The arrival of Eliza and, later, Higgins' instructions concerning Eliza allow Mrs. Pearce to make pertinent observations about Higgins' deportment, manners, language, and conduct. When she announces that a very common girl is at the door, we know immediately, from Higgins' reaction, that he is a bit eccentric. When he begins his dealings with Eliza, for example, he sees her not as a human being but as a "bit of baggage." In contrast, Colonel Pickering is more tender and solicitous. At one point, he reminds Higgins that the girl might have some sensitive feelings, despite her "guttersnipe" exterior. This basic contrast between the two men will continue throughout the drama.

Eliza's reactions during this first visit by her father is indicative of her character. As is consistent with her class, she believes that if she can *pay* for the lesson, then Higgins *has* to be polite to her. Furthermore, she is determined that she shall not be cheated (her offer of a suitable fee for an hour's lesson is, to her, very serious; of course, to us and to Higgins, it is comic); as the scene progresses, Eliza is wary of Higgins; she is suspicious of being mistreated, drugged, seduced, or rejected.

After Higgins decides that he will accept the challenge of teaching Eliza to become a lady, two matters emerge. First, Mrs. Pearce wonders "what is to become of her when you've finished your teaching? You must look ahead a little." This is the ultimate question for a practical woman, and it is a question repeated later by Higgins' mother. At the end of the play, it becomes the central point in Eliza's revolt from Higgins. Never during the course of the play does he seriously consider what is to be done with Eliza. Here, for example, he merely says that when he is done with her, "we can throw her back into the gutter." This view, however, will become the main topic for Eliza's later consideration, for by that time she will be trained in such a way that she will no longer be able to function in the gutter. Thus, already Higgins is insensitive and blind to his moral responsibility to another human being. The second matter involves not merely Higgins' teaching Eliza how to pronounce words correctly, but in teaching her the proper words to use and also the proper grammatical form. This concern will also prove to be the essence of the comedy in the next scene, when Eliza will narrate a story about the death of her aunt with *impeccable* pronunciation, but her choice of subject matter will be deliciously low and vulgar.

The original Pygmalion theme is now fully introduced. The creator, Higgins (Pygmalion) has found his stone Galatea in the person of Eliza (this sack of baggage, this squashed cabbage) — whom he will "carve" and mold into a great duchess, someone whom he can control and command.

When Mrs. Pearce takes Eliza away, we are hardly prepared for the immediate appearance of her father. The audience and Higgins alike expect an irate father, anxious over the safety of his youthful daughter; we expect him to demand honorable protection for his offspring. Alfred Doolittle, however, is just the opposite — and he is also one of Shaw's most delightful creations. At the time of Doolittle's appearance, Mrs. Pearce has been lecturing Higgins on manners and etiquette: if Eliza is to be in the house, Higgins must watch his language, stop appearing in house robes, cease wiping his hands on his clothes, refrain from cursing, and begin performing other acts of proper manners. With the appearance of Doolittle, the questions of social manners become parodied. The subject is replaced by the idea of social morality and especially middle-class morality (or low-class morality).

As noted above, when Doolittle first appears, we expect the virtuous father, and we see the hypocritical blackmailer. When the blackmail plot is obviously going to fail, we are exposed to Doolittle's supposedly righteous indignation, then we see it fade, and he becomes an unscrupulous and ingratiating pimp, willing to sell off his daughter's virtue for a mere pittance. Again, his bumbling attempts fail. But by now, Higgins is attracted to the resourcefulness of this intended blackmailer and to Doolittle's picturesque language; when Higgins demands an answer from Doolittle, the old man's rhetorical retort pleases Higgins. Doolittle says: "I'm willing to tell you. I'm wanting to tell you. I'm waiting to tell you." For Higgins, and for Shaw (who likes to take digs wherever possible), this sentimental rhetoric accounts for the Welsh dialect and also for Doolittle's mendacity and dishonesty.

When all else fails, thus, Doolittle resorts to speaking the plain truth, but it is a truth so original that it captures the imagination of both Higgins and Pickering. Whereas most charity goes to the "deserving poor," Doolittle dispenses with traditional morality and charity; he argues for some consideration of the *undeserving poor*; in a fanciful flight of philosophical oratory, Doolittle maintains that his type of people has been ignored, and it is now time to contribute money to someone like him who will take the money, go out on a weekend binge, spend it all on booze, and then be ready to go back to his miserable job on Monday. He maintains that he too has a right to this type of debauch, and yet he has been denied it by the narrow-minded prejudices of middle-class morality.

Higgins is so taken aback by this unique, bizarre logic that he offers to give Doolittle ten pounds, but Doolittle rapidly rejects this offer because that large a sum would entail middle-class responsibility, whereas the smaller sum would be just enough to go out on a binge with no regrets and no responsibilities. The irony of Doolittle's logic is that at the end of the play, Doolittle will be forced to accept middle-class responsibilities and morality because by then he will have inherited enough money that he will be encumbered for the rest of his life and will have to forever abandon his free and easy ways as a member of the "undeserving poor."

With Eliza's re-entry on the stage, Shaw returns to his social criticism. Eliza's father doesn't recognize his daughter because he "never thought she would clean up as good looking as that. . . . She's a credit to me, aint she?" Since Shaw didn't believe in a genuine poor class, he is making a gentle point that the possession of "hot and cold water" and "woolly towels," soft brushes, and soap can make a ragamuffin look entirely different. This scene emphasizes the basic difference between Eliza and her father: Doolittle likes being a part of the "undeserving poor," while Eliza yearns, above all, to escape from this class and to join the respectable middle class. This is the reason why she has come to Higgins: to take lessons in order to escape the stigma of her class. We are now able to review what we have read and see the significance of Eliza's howling when Higgins says that if Eliza misbehaves they will simply throw her in the dustbin—that is, her father's job is collecting the ashes and refuse of dust bins, and since he has already thrown Eliza out many years ago, she has no desire to be "collected" by him again. In fact, at the end of the drama, one of the options that is open to Eliza is that she can return to her father, but she resolutely refuses to do so. And at the end of this particular act, Eliza shows her first bit of humorous class snobbism: now that she is clean, she would like to ride back to her old district and parade in front of her old cronies and lord it over them now that she "has risen in the world."

ACT III

Summary

This act opens in Mrs. Higgins' drawing room on the day that she is receiving guests. She is frustrated and upset to find that her son has paid a call on her during her "at-home day." He promised her never to come when she had company because he and his manners always offend her guests. Today is no exception. He distresses his mother immediately by telling her that he has invited a girl to call on her, a girl whom he "picked up" and taught to speak properly in the matter of only a short time. Higgins wants his mother to notice not only *how* the girl pronounces her words, but also *what* she pronounces as she speaks.

The parlor maid enters and announces the arrival of Mrs. and Miss Eynsford-Hill, whose accents Higgins remembers, but he cannot remember where he actually met them. After introductions, Colonel Pickering is shown in, and then he is followed shortly by Freddy Eynsford-Hill. Higgins is delighted that the company has expanded so that Eliza will be better tested in front of a moderately large group. After some brief exchanges, Miss Doolittle is announced, and Eliza, exquisitely dressed, enters with remarkable poise and distinction, exuding an air of complete self-possession. She has been warned to speak about only two subjects—the weather and health. (This will be especially comic later when she does indeed confine herself to the topic of her aunt's health, but her aunt's health is indeed bizarre.)

As Eliza is introduced, she greets each person with an elaborate "How do you do"; her pronunciation is uttered with impeccable precision. When the subject of the weather is mentioned, Eliza volunteers her observations in such an erudite and precise manner that it astonishes everyone. To the simple question, "Do you think it will rain?" Eliza answers: "The shallow depression in the west of these islands is likely to move slowly in an easterly direction. There are no indications of any great change in the barometrical situation."

Having exhausted the subject of the weather, she thus ventures onto her other restricted subject – health – and announces the circumstances surrounding her aunt's death in the most precise English. The precision of her diction, of course, only heightens the lurid aspects of her aunt's death as Eliza narrates her tale in perfectly enunciated slang terms from the slums, exposing all of the bizarre and extraordinary aspects of her aunt's death. Higgins tries to cover some of Eliza's mistakes by referring to her language as the "new small talk," but Freddy, however, is delighted with the entire performance. He is clearly anxious to hear more and to accompany Miss Doolittle home, but Eliza, noticing Higgins' "Ahems," announces that she must go, that she must catch a taxi. "Suffering from shock" (Shaw's phrase), Mrs. Eynsford-Hill sighs, "Well, I really can't get used to the new ways."

After Eliza leaves, Mrs. Eynsford-Hill continues to expound on the younger generation's way of talking, and her daughter Clara maintains that it is really quite up-to-date to talk in such a manner. Higgins mischievously encourages the young lady to try out some of the new slang on some of her mother's friends.

After the Eynsford-Hills leave, Higgins is exhilarated about Eliza's performance, but his mother points out that Eliza is not yet presentable – that is, Eliza is merely a "triumph of your art and of her dressmaker's," but that she reveals her social origins in every sentence that she speaks. Part of the trouble, she says, is that Eliza is adopting Henry's mode of speech, a mode which is acceptable on a canal barge, but one which is not proper for a garden party.

Mrs. Higgins then inquires into the nature of the household arrangement, or more specifically, where does Eliza live? Higgins bluntly and openly confesses, "With us, of course." Mrs. Higgins then points out to the two men a problem that neither of them has considered: what is to be done with Eliza after they have finished their little experiment? They are giving Eliza "the manners and habits that disqualify a fine lady from earning her own living without giving her a fine lady's income." Soon Eliza will be so well trained and be such a lady that no one will hire her, and she will have nothing to live on – and no job. Mrs. Higgins is assured by both men that there is nothing to worry about; they will do whatever is right by her. After all, Eliza is such a mimic that she keeps them constantly laughing by her imitations of other people's accents and affectations. As her son and his friend leave, Mrs. Higgins returns impatiently and angrily to her work at her writing table, but she cannot concentrate. "Oh, men! ! men! ! men! !" she exclaims.

Commentary

Between Act II and Act III, an undisclosed amount of time has elapsed, enough time to allow Eliza to master some of the basics of pronunciation but not enough time for her to master proper subject matter or the theme of discussion. When she appears at Mrs. Higgins', there is an obvious contrast. No longer is she the flighty Eliza of the first two acts; now, she is the reserved Eliza; she is "exquisitely dressed," and she "produces an impression of such remarkable distinction and beauty" that everyone is quite taken aback. The contrast on stage has to be tremendous or else the Eynsford-Hills would recognize her as the flower girl from the encounter in the first act. Accordingly, we, the audience, are delighted that they are so inept that they do not recognize her. The new Eliza seemingly fits in well in these new contrasting surroundings; that is, Mrs. Higgins' drawing room is described as being very formal with exquisitely refined furniture of the Chippendale style, furnished with excellent oil paintings and other art objects. Thus, the artificial formality of Eliza's speech blends well with the stiff formality of the highly decorative setting.

Following through with the Pygmalion legend, this act shows us Pygmalion's work of art – his Galatea of mythology – emerging in the figure of Eliza. Here is the beginning of the artistic creation making her first appearance, and everything about the creation suggests that it will be, in its finished form, a true masterpiece. Even at this point, Freddy Eynsford-Hill is totally smitten by Eliza's beauty and her superb uniqueness.

At the beginning of the act, the relationship between Mrs. Higgins and her son is humorous because the mother's attitude toward her son is so eccentric and because she expresses herself with as much forthright honesty as does her son. The depiction of Mrs. Higgins is that of an excellent personality filled with tolerance, intelligence, and imagination. Like Mrs. Pearce, she is immediately concerned over the fate of this "living doll" that Higgins has created. This depiction is important because Shaw maintains later in his epilogue that one of the reasons for Eliza's rejection of the possibility of marriage to Higgins is that she could never live up to Mrs. Higgins' standards, that she could never equal Mrs. Higgins' grasp of life.

Part of the dramatic humor of this act lies in the fact that we, the audience, know who the Eynsford-Hills are, but that Professor Higgins can't remember where *he* might have seen them, which makes us superior to the very superior Higgins. Throughout the scene, Higgins lives up to Mrs. Higgins' expectations – that is, he is too outspoken, "rather trying on more commonplace occasions," he uses improper language, and, in general, he has an amazing lack of manners.

With Higgins' failure in the realm of manners, we are then presented to Eliza, who will now perform in this same setting. Higgins has, we hear, coached her on not only *how* to pronounce her words, but also on "what she pronounces." This anticipates Eliza's vulgar narration of the death of her aunt. This scene, with Eliza demonstrating her newly acquired knowledge, is the central scene of this act. It is in this scene, while Eliza is discussing the weather, that both in the film version and in the musical comedy version, Eliza pronounces her now-famous line: "The rain in Spain stays mainly in the plain." The comedy of this scene relies upon the contrast between Eliza's *mode* of speech and her *subject matter*. She has been trained to pronounce words with impeccable perfection, but as Higgins feared, she has not learned what is proper to discuss and what is not. Higgins thought wrongly that he was safe in confining her subject to the weather and to one's health. It is, of course, humorously comic that Eliza does confine herself to these two supposedly safe subjects, but naively, she narrates some rather bizarre details of her aunt's death, using the terminology of the slums, yet pronouncing the unsavory words with complete precision. Her enun-ciation of improper words makes the entire narration comically in-congruous. As a result, behind the outward, new facade of Eliza lies an uncarved interior which remains on the vulgar side.

In spite of the squalid, if beautifully spoken, narration of her aunt's death, Eliza possesses an element of sincerity in contrast to the silly affectation of Miss Clara Eynsford-Hill's attempt to dupli-cate the "new manner of small talk." After Eliza leaves, Mrs. Eynsford-Hill asserts that she cannot become accustomed to young ladies using such words as "bloody," "beastly," and "filthy," and so forth. Actually, Shaw himself was put off by "proper" young ladies, such as Clara, attempting to use common expressions; he once main-tained that "a flower girl's conversation is much more picturesque, [and has] much better rhetoric, [is] much more concise, interesting, and arresting than the conversation of the drawing-room, and that the moment she begins to speak beautifully she gains an advantage by the intensity of her experience and the strength of her feeling about it."

After Eliza departs, Mrs. Higgins also comments on the dispari-ty between Eliza's speech and her subject matter. As noted, part of Eliza's problem is that she is learning the English language anew from Professor Henry Higgins, who (despite the fact that he is a pro-fessor) uses speech which is not fit for the drawing room. Mrs. Hig-gins then returns to Shaw's original Pygmalion theme when she points out that Eliza is a triumph of Higgins' art and the art of the dressmaker; but that Eliza is not yet a presentable person. She is only partially carved. The thrill of the experiment for Higgins is also part of the Pygmalion theme; as he tells his mother: "You have no idea how frightfully interesting it is to take a human being and change her into a quite different human being by creating a new speech for her." Higgins, then, is clearly the artist, Pygmalion, and Eliza is Galatea: the only difference between life and the myth is that here the artist is *not* falling in love with his creation and, ultimately, he will not be able to control his own creation. Ultimately, Eliza will have a soul and a will of her own, completely independent of her creator. At present, however, her creator is content to be amused by his creation since Eliza loves to mimic all sorts of people, especially all of these people after she, Higgins, and Pickering return home.

ACT IV

Summary

Act IV begins some time later and takes place in Higgins' laboratory-living room. The scene opens on the night after there has earlier been a great success where Eliza was presented as a duchess at an ambassador's garden party, as was stipulated in the original wager between Higgins and Pickering. Eliza has been a smashing success. Thus, when the scene opens, Higgins and Pickering are celebrating their triumph. (By this time, the actual financial terms of the wager are insignificant; Pickering has helped train Eliza and is sharing in the triumph, even though he has lost the wager.)

Eliza enters; she is brilliantly dressed in impeccable taste but her "expression is almost tragic." Immediately, Higgins begins to look for his slippers, and he is so busy congratulating himself on his great success that he is unaware that Eliza has left the room and has returned with his slippers; to fetch Higgins' slippers is apparently another accepted aspect of her training.

As Higgins and Pickering sit down and discuss the great triumph of the day, we hear that Eliza has been a tremendous success not only at the garden party, but also at the dinner party and at the opera later. Higgins then admits that after the first few minutes, it became obviously apparent that he was going to easily win his bet with Pickering, and, as a result, he was bored for the rest of the time. In contrast, Pickering rather enjoyed himself, especially the very professional manner in which Eliza carried the entire charade off. Pickering then retires for the evening, followed by Higgins, yelling to Eliza to put out the lights.

Alone, Eliza gives vent to her pent-up fury as she flings herself furiously onto the floor, raging. At that moment, Higgins returns, looking for his slippers, which Eliza hurls at him with all her force. He is totally baffled by her display of anger. He is furthermore astounded by her calling him a "selfish brute" who is ready to throw her back into the gutter now that she has won his bet for him. Higgins is dumbfounded at her presumptuous claim; he refuses to acknowledge that *she* had anything to do with his winning the bet. The entire feat was accomplished by *his* coaching and *his* brilliance. When she physically attacks him, asking what is to become of her, Higgins restrains her and says, "What does it matter what becomes of you?" Higgins' brusqueness, however, subsides, and he relents enough to question her about her anxieties and to offer a glass of champagne to relieve the strain of the day. He assures her that she will feel better now that the garden party is over. Eliza's concerns, however, clearly and seriously involve the future. She asks: "What am I fit for? What have you left me fit for? Where am I to go? What am I to do? What's to become of me?" Even though both Mrs. Pearce and Mrs. Higgins have warned Higgins about this dilemma, he has obviously never given it a moment's thought. He can't imagine that she will have any difficulty in finding something to do—or even in marrying someone. After all, not all men are "confirmed old bachelors" like Higgins and Pickering. Maybe Mrs. Higgins could find a young chap for her. Eliza then informs him that all that she has ever done is sell flowers; now, as a lady, she can't even sell flowers; all she can hope to do is sell herself. She wishes Higgins had left her where he found her. (She has apparently forgotten that *she* came to see *Higgins*—not the other way around.)

Higgins returns to Eliza's original desire to work in a flower shop, and he suggests that Pickering could perhaps set up Eliza in her own shop. Higgins thinks this solution settles everything, and once again, looking for his slippers, he prepares to retire. But Eliza has one more question. She wants to know what clothes belong to her, personally—that is, what clothes may she keep and what clothes belong to the "experiment." After all, Higgins and Pickering might need some of the clothes for the next girl they pick up to experiment on. She reminds Higgins of her past: "I'm only a common ignorant girl; and in *my* station I have to be careful." Higgins tells her that she can take all the clothes, but she cannot have the jewelry; it was rented. She antagonizes him further by asking him to take the jewelry to his room so there will be no "risk of their being missing." She also returns a ring which he bought her, but he throws the ring so angrily into the fireplace that Eliza crouches over the piano, her hands over her face, crying, "Don't you hit me." Higgins now feels wounded, and when Eliza tells him that he had better leave a note for Mrs. Pearce because she (Eliza) won't do his errands any more, he leaves, slamming the door savagely and calling Eliza "a heartless guttersnipe." Alone, Eliza senses her triumph over the master; thus, she quickly kneels and digs the ring out of the ashes. She finds it, considers it for a moment, then flings it down and goes upstairs in a rage.

Commentary

This act presents the completion of the artist's masterpiece; here is the fully realized Galatea that Pygmalion created in the form of the living Eliza. Here, we see a person completely transformed from the "guttersnipe" that we saw in Covent Garden in the first act. At the beginning of the act, both Pickering and Higgins are so absorbed in their own triumph that both fail to realize that the success of the experiment belongs as much to Eliza as it does to their teaching. In fact, when Eliza suggests that she won their bet for them, Higgins repudiates her claim vehemently: "*You* won my bet! You! Presumptuous insect! *I* won it." What neither Pickering nor Higgins takes into account is the stupendous effort that Eliza herself has contributed to the entire endeavor. As we shall see in the next act, Mrs. Higgins certainly recognizes Eliza's contribution, but both men are so absorbed in their own achievement that they fail to grasp the fact that Eliza has worked exceedingly hard to be able to speak like a lady; as a result, she developed an intense devotion and loyalty towards her two masters—not a *love* devotion but a deep and sincere devotion and also a strong desire to please. Thus, at the beginning of this act, when the men ignore her, her pent-up fury turns to rage. The image which Shaw uses is that of a well-trained puppy dog fetching its master's slippers. At the beginning of the act, Eliza does, in fact, fetch Higgins' slippers. The men, however, fail to pet and admire the "puppy" for her achievements, and therefore the trained puppy turns on its masters. In the next act, this image of the trained dog fetching slippers will be continued and will be developed as a central metaphor. Here, the slippers are dropped, literally, by having Eliza throw them at the master. However much Eliza has changed outwardly, this act of rage aligns her with the Eliza of Covent Garden of the first act.

In the original myth, Pygmalion had to pray to the gods to give his creation a soul. What Higgins as a creative artist did not realize was that his Galatea had a soul already. He has been able to polish the outside to a high degree of mechanical perfection, but he failed to note that at the same time, his creation was developing an inner soul and a mind of her own.

Whereas Mrs. Pearce's and Mrs. Higgins' first concern was what would happen to Eliza after the transformation, this has now become a question of major importance for Eliza. In a conventional type of romantic comedy, the ending would probably show the total success of the experiment with the audience leaving the theater with the knowledge of Eliza's triumph at the ambassador's party and with Eliza and her master's falling in love, just as it happened in the myth. However, Shaw was interested in what happened *after* the triumph. And Eliza herself asks, what is she fit for, and where is she to go, and what will become of her? Higgins has been so completely involved with his experiment and the success of it that this question has never seriously entered his mind. Even now, when it is pointed out to him, he cannot take it seriously. Eliza knows that she absolutely cannot return to her old way of making a living, for she is now trained to be a lady and has no visible means to support herself in the position for which she is now trained. Thus Higgins has created a work of art without considering what he will do with this work of art after its exhibit is over. When Higgins suggests some sort of marriage, Shaw is making another dig at social standards. That is, when Eliza was a flower girl, she sold flowers and not her person; now that she is Lady Eliza, she can't sell flowers anymore (that would be beneath her) but she *can* sell herself.

At the end of the act, Eliza needles Higgins in a desperate attempt to break through his outer veneer. In her own repressed emotions, she wants to see him hurt—just like she has been hurt; she wants to penetrate the god-like distance that Higgins surrounds himself with; thus, she taunts him until she makes him lose his temper, and she is able to enjoy the spectacle of a so-called, self-proclaimed god losing his self-control—that is, Higgins is a "god" now made human, with human emotions and fury.

ACT V

Summary

This act returns to Mrs. Higgins' drawing room as the parlor maid comes in to tell Mrs. Higgins that the Professor and the

Colonel are downstairs telephoning the police and that Mr. Henry is "in a state." Mrs. Higgins sends word upstairs to Eliza to remain in her room until she sends for her. Higgins enters, loudly proclaiming Eliza's disappearance, which has distracted his entire routine since he has relied on her to keep up his appointment book for him. Mrs. Higgins is expressing her disapproval of their having informed the police when the maid announces the arrival of Mr. Doolittle, whom she describes as being a gentleman dressed brilliantly in a new frock coat and other elegant attire. He enters and begins immediately accusing Higgins of being responsible for his present affluent condition; that is, he has come into a very large amount of money which has forced him to become *respectable*. It has, he says, "ruined me. Destroyed my happiness. Tied me up and delivered me into the hands of middle-class morality." It seems that for a joke, Higgins mentioned Doolittle's name to a wealthy American as being "the most original moralist at present in England," and, as a result, the American, in his will, left an immense trust fund to Doolittle if he would lecture six times a year on moral reforms. As a result, Doolittle has lost his free and easy ways and is now forced to conform to middle-class morality, along with its confining respectability. The sum is so large that Doolittle is intimidated and can't properly give it up. Mrs. Higgins is pleased and sees now that Eliza can return home and live with her father in his new wealthy status, but Higgins protests strongly that he bought Eliza for five pounds and that Doolittle can't interfere unless he is a rogue, which Doolittle readily admits that he is – that is, he's part honest and part rogue, "a little of both . . . like the rest of us."

Mrs. Higgins then informs them that Eliza is upstairs, but before she is to be sent for, Higgins must promise to behave. Mrs. Higgins then reprimands both Higgins and Pickering for being so completely self-centered and inconsiderate of Eliza's feelings. She asks Doolittle to retire for a moment until Eliza becomes reconciled with Higgins and Pickering. Eliza enters and addresses the two men in a refined, distant, and assured manner. Her dignified carriage and her ease of manner unnerves Higgins, who immediately attempts to treat her as his "property," as something he created "out of the squashed cabbage leaves of Covent Garden." Eliza, however, does not allow Higgins to rattle her by his insulting manners; instead, she thanks Colonel Pickering for his having always treated her as a lady and never as a guttersnipe. She says furthermore that everything that she has learned about manners has been due to the Colonel, and she now realizes that it is not what a person *does*, but how she is *treated* that makes her a lady: "The difference between a lady and a flower girl is not how she behaves, but how she's treated. I shall always be a flower girl to Professor Higgins, because he always treats me as a flower girl, and always will, but I know I can be a lady to you, because you always treat me as a lady, and always will." She learned grammar and pronunciation from Professor Higgins, but it was from Colonel Pickering that she learned self-respect. When she refuses to return to Wimpole Street, Higgins predicts that she will "relapse into the gutter in three weeks" without him. Eliza, however, says that she could not utter the old sounds if she tried and, at that moment, her father, Mr. Doolittle, appears at the window in all his splendid attire, and Eliza spontaneously emits one of her old guttural sounds—"A-a-a-a-ah-ow-ooh!"—an exclamation that utterly delights and vindicates Higgins.

Doolittle has come to announce his marriage and to ask Eliza to attend the wedding; he explains that, like himself, his common-law wife has also been defeated by middle-class morality: "respectability has broke all the spirit out of her." When Eliza goes upstairs to get ready to accompany her father to his wedding, Doolittle confesses that he is nervous because he has never been married before—not even to Eliza's mother—but he has never told this to Eliza. Mrs. Higgins says that she will also attend the wedding with Eliza, and Pickering leaves with the bridegroom.

As Eliza is about to leave, Higgins blocks the doorway. He says that he wants Eliza to come back, but he will *not* change his manners, which he maintains are *exactly* the same as the Colonel's. Eliza disagrees: "That's not true," she says, "He treats a flower girl as if she was a duchess." To which Higgins replies, "And I treat a duchess as if she was a flower girl." Higgins continues, maintaining that good manners or bad manners are not important; instead, it is more important to have the same manners for all people. If he has treated her badly, she has to admit that she has never seen him treat someone else differently or better. He is proud that she is now independent—in fact, it's one of the basic things that he has wanted her to learn—but he insists that he can get along quite well without her, even though he admits: "I have grown accustomed to your voice and appearance." Eliza then reminds him that he has both her voice and her "appearance" in numerous photographs and recordings; when he feels lonesome, he can turn on one of his recordings of her. Higgins counters, however, that he can't turn her "soul" on, and he says, furthermore, that he values quality more than service, and he points out that Eliza cannot buy a claim on him "by fetching my slippers and my spectacles." In fact, her "little dog's tricks of fetching and carrying slippers" can in no way compare to the greatness of his creation – that is, the Duchess Eliza.

At this point, Eliza is absolutely confused as to what course her life is to take. She sorely regrets the loss of independence which she once had. Higgins offers to adopt her or settle money on her, but he is horrified when he hears that Freddy Eynsford-Hill is romantically interested in her; Freddy, Higgins says, can't *make* anything of" her. Eliza responds that maybe she can do something for Freddy; after all, she only wants to be natural, and she wants a little kindness, which Freddy can certainly give to her. She knows that she cannot return to her old way of life, and she cannot stand the idea of living "with a low common man after you two" (Higgins and Pickering); and she certainly doesn't intend to go to her father's house to live; thus, as soon as possible, she will marry Freddy.

Higgins is horrified at her conclusion, and he loudly asserts, "I'm not going to have my masterpiece thrown away on Freddy." But Eliza is determined to have her independence, and therefore she decides that she will teach. What in heaven's name will she teach, Higgins asks, and he is totally astonished when she announces that she will teach *phonetics*. She reminds him what a good ear she has, and, furthermore, she has more manners than he has and, therefore, she will be able to advertise and can thus become financially independent. Eliza is no longer frightened of Higgins, and she defies him to strike her. Suddenly Higgins reverses himself; he admires her for her independence: her defiance is far "better than fetching slippers and finding spectacles." But even after she has asserted her independence, Higgins assumes that she will decide to return to Wimpole Street and they – Higgins, Pickering, and Eliza – will be "three old bachelors," together instead their living together formerly as, in Higgins' words, "two men and a silly girl." At that moment, Mrs. Higgins returns to say that Eliza's carriage is waiting. Higgins, who knows that he cannot behave himself in church, has decided to

stay behind, and so Eliza bids him goodbye, saying that they will
not see each other again. Higgins ignores this comment and, instead, he gives Eliza some errands to do on the way home. Eliza
disdainfully leaves, telling him to buy the gloves and the tie himself.
Mrs. Higgins fears that Henry has spoiled the girl, and she
volunteers to do his errands, but Higgins is confident that Eliza will
buy them herself.

Commentary

Act V presents the fully realized Galatea, the creation of the artist, alive in all of her splendor. The "romance" of the play's subtitle
refers, of course, to the complete transformation of the
"guttersnipe," the "squashed cabbage leaf" of the first act, into this
delightful creature who is more magnificent than any real
duchess – more real because, as it develops during the course of this
act, Eliza has manners which are better and more polished than
most duchesses. Furthermore, unlike the original Liza, the flower
girl, this new Eliza has learned to control her emotional outbursts
completely; now, her calculated calm and her poised reserve cause
the normally self-contained and super-rational Higgins to lose his
temper. We can now say confidently that the work of art has become
superior to the creator.

The opening of the act implies that the creator, Higgins, could
never conceive of the fact that his creation would, of her own voli-
tion, walk out on him. His colossal conceit (an assessment that is
supported by Colonel Pickering) makes Higgins assume that Eliza
has been kidnapped or that something horrible has happened that
will require notifying the police. His colossal ego will not or cannot
entertain the idea that she might have now gained enough independence to strike out on her own. In fact, it is not until the end of the act
that Higgins finally recognizes that the work of art is now independent of its creator and is thus separate from him; she has no further need of him. Therefore, for any but the most sentimental
readers, there is nothing in these acts that could possibly suggest a
romantic entanglement between the two. Higgins will never accept
Eliza as an equal; he will always try to bully her, even though he
says that he likes her better now that she no longer fetches his slippers and spectacles. Eliza, having learned that manners involve not

only her own conduct but also how other people treat her, could never become involved with a man who constantly treats her as though she were a flower girl.

This act also shows the comical transformation of Alfred Doolittle. Earlier, he was completely content to be a member of the "undeserving poor," and he took special delight in ridiculing and flouting the morals of the middle class. Now he is thrust completely into this morality, which necessitates that he obey some of their dreadful conventions, such as dressing properly and marrying the woman with whom he has been living. It has, as he feared earlier, placed him in a position of responsibility and it has, therefore, destroyed his cherished independence. Whereas earlier he was frightened to accept ten pounds rather than five pounds because ten might necessitate some degree of responsibility, now he is in control of an immense sum and, consequently, the dreadful poor will be badgering him constantly for handouts. Now he fears that not only will he have to marry, but that he might have to help support Eliza, whom he threw out over two years ago. He can even tell Higgins: "Have some consideration for my feelings as a middle-class man." Thus, with this inverted statement, Doolittle has sunk completely into the horrible complacency of middle-class morality.

At the end of the play, the two opposing forces are clearly before us: Higgins ends up so devoted to improving mankind *in general* that he lacks the ability to be decent to a single member of mankind, to a fine human being such as Eliza. He can teach her to be a magnificent duchess, a Galatea, a work of art, but he lacks sufficient tact in their personal relationship to avoid constantly hurting her feelings. In his devotion to reforming the entire human race, he trods innocently and unmercifully on a single individual human being. When Eliza remarks that she will *not* be walked on, Higgins answers her in his usual bullying fashion: "Then get out of my way; for I wont stop for you."

Even though Higgins has "grown accustomed to [her] face and voice," it is only because they are convenient pieces to be used, but he can get along without them. Thus the central conflict of the play is now stated: Higgins is the crusading scientist who is determined to save the world, even though he might have to hurt those closest to him. Eliza, on the other hand, wishes to be the recipient of a little loving kindness, and if it means marrying Freddy Eynsford-Hill in order to find this human companionship and warmth, then she will do so.

Consequently, with the conflict clearly stated for Higgins, the essence of human life is through mutual improvement; for Eliza, it is through human loving and commitment—then only the most sloppy, sentimental reader could ever think that their relationship will ever change.

SEQUEL

When the play ends, the audience is left to ponder what will happen to the characters later; for the sentimentalist, it is a foregone conclusion that Higgins and Eliza will probably marry, even though there is ample indication in the play that they will not. Thus, in the prose "Sequel," Shaw reasserts his premise that such a wedding between Higgins and Eliza is absolutely impossible, and he explains again that he subtitled his play a "romance" because the technical meaning of "romance" refers to anything that was highly improbable; for example, the transformation of a flower girl into a duchess in six months is indeed highly improbable. A romance, however, also can suggest a "happy ending," and Shaw says he is *not* interested in such an ending to his story. He will not allow his creation, Eliza, to marry such a misfit as Higgins simply to satisfy the whims of the sentimentalists of the world, even though these sentimental people outnumber the realists. First of all, Eliza is beautiful, and she is now also intelligent, desirable, and witty enough to find a husband closer to her own age; after all, Higgins is over twenty years her senior. Eliza herself also knows that she is young enough to find someone much more desirable than Higgins. Second, Eliza recognizes that Mrs. Higgins is the model mother—that is, she is a woman of unusual charm and intelligence, and she possesses a tolerance for Higgins' idiosyncratic manners, while sweetly disapproving of them. Eliza is now intelligent enough to know she would be a rival to this "irresistible wealthy" woman. Third, Eliza does not want to be a "second fiddle" to Higgins' study of phonetics and the English language; she knows that Higgins' experiments will always come first, and she would have to be content with being second place in his life. Last, Eliza, once having gained her independence, simply has no desire to be constantly combatting Higgins' wit, his resentment, his bullying, and the condescendingly superior way which he takes with her. Higgins would always remind her of her origins and would attempt to evade her anger after he had bullied her. Thus, she reasons, why not marry Freddy Eynsford-Hill? He worships her, and he would always treat her as a lady. But Freddy is not equipped to earn a living, and Mrs. Eynsford-Hill could not offer them financial assistance. Eliza's father has risen so socially high in the world that he spends all he has to keep up his appearance and, therefore, cannot be of financial assistance to them. Consequently, Colonel Pickering again comes to the rescue and sets them up in a flower shop, a move which violates Mrs. Eynsford-Hill's concept that people in trade are inferior people. Unfortunately, neither Eliza, who only sold flowers for a pittance earlier, nor Freddy has the slightest concept of how to run a shop, and thus the Colonel has to constantly rescue them from economic disaster. Through it all, Higgins is delighted that Freddy is a failure; it justifies his opinion of the young man. But by attending night school, by hiring outside help, by luck, and by adding food items for sale, the shop began to prosper.

Eliza is still a part of Wimpole Street, she is still interested vaguely in Higgins, but she keeps him at a distance and holds his derisions of Freddy to a minimum. She is also very much beloved by Colonel Pickering, and she returns his love. In Shaw's words, Eliza "likes Freddy and she likes the Colonel; and she does not like Higgins and Mr. Doolittle. Galatea never does quite like Pygmalion: his relation to her is too godlike to be altogether agreeable."

CHARACTER ANALYSES

Professor Henry Higgins

Henry Higgins, forty years old, is a bundle of paradoxes. In spite of his brilliant intellectual achievements, his manners are usually those of the worst sort of petulant, whining child. He is a combination of loveable eccentricities, brilliant achievements, and devoted dedication to improving the human race. Yet he is completely socially inept; his manners are so bad that his own mother does not want him in her house when she has company, and his manners are so offensive that she will not attend the same church at the same time. Since manners have always been the subject matter of comedies from the time of Aristophanes, Higgins' view of manners differs greatly from his own actions. His use of phonetics to make a flower girl into a duchess does not mean that the play is about phonetics; the play concerns different definitions of manners, and thus Higgins' actions must be taken fully into account.

Henry Higgins is a confirmed bachelor, and this fact alone should rule out all popularizers who would create a romantic entanglement between Higgins and Eliza. In addition, he is so set in his ways that he announces to Eliza that if someone doesn't want to get run over, they had better get out of his way. To accomplish his aims, he will trample on anyone's feelings – whether that person be a flower girl in Covent Garden or a real duchess or a lady in his mother's elaborate drawing room. Thus, one of Higgins' claims to equality is not that he doesn't have manners (it is a foregone conclusion that he has none), but that he treats all people alike. However, he only *thinks* that he does; he is not as egalitarian and democratic as he likes to think that he is. When Higgins first meets Eliza in Covent Garden and is taking down her vocal sounds, he is extremely clever – so clever, in fact, that his horribly bad manners are accepted by the audience as being clever. In his tirade against Eliza, when he vents his wrath against her, we tend, on first hearing his tirade, to forgive him because he has such an admirable command of the English language as he simply rips to pieces a "guttersnipe" and "a squashed cabbage leaf." Note his superb language: "A woman who utters such depressing and disgusting sounds has no right to be anywhere – no right to live. Remember that you are a human being with a soul and the divine gift of articulate speech . . . don't sit there crooning like a bilious pigeon." Anyone who can deliver such splendid invective is admired for his or her brilliant, spontaneous use of the English language, and especially when it is directed against so lowly a person as this flower girl from the slums. But in a play dealing with manners, no proper gentleman would utter such condemnations. Later, we find out that Colonel Pickering treated Eliza properly from the very first. Thus, in spite of Higgins' claiming to treat all people with the same manners, he certainly does not treat Mrs. Eynsford-Hill and Clara with such a display of invective, and both of these characters represent everything that Higgins abhors; they represent the worst sort of upper-middle-class hypocrisy that both he and Doolittle despise. But in spite of his bad manners, Higgins *is* clever, and we do admire his cleverness, even at the expense of a flower girl.

Why else do we like Higgins? Because he is Shaw's creative rebel who floats through many of Shaw's dramas. Higgins rejects middle-class moralities. He admires do-nothing Doolittles for their honesty in asserting that they are the undeserving poor; he will devote his scientific skill to changing a flower girl into a duchess; he is ultimately interested in the soul of his creation (Eliza-Galatea) and not in her pronunciation; and he is devoted to improving the human race by his own scientific methods. And, last, we cannot deny his charm: Mrs. Pearce, his housekeeper, has often threatened to leave because of Henry's atrocious manners (improper language, improper dress, bad table behavior, etc.), but she is always charmed by him into remaining with him. Ultimately, Eliza is also so charmed by her association with Higgins (and Pickering) that she does not want to live with someone else. But if Higgins is charming, he is also a tyrannical bully; if he is devastatingly intelligent, he is also ignorantly insensitive to the feelings of others; if he is god-like in his achievements, he is childishly petulant in his wanting his own way; if he believes in his scientific methodology, he is also something of the intuitive poet; and if he is a man so confident of his aim in life, he is also a man so ignorant of his own personality that he really thinks himself timid, modest, and diffident. Thus, his appeal remains partly in the many contradictions that he is heir to.

Eliza Doolittle

Shaw's story of the flower girl from the slums who was taught to speak so properly that she was able to pass as a duchess at an ambassador's garden party is perhaps one of the best known works by Shaw—partly because of the popularity of the play which, in turn, inspired a more sentimentalized version in a popular movie and, later, became one of the world's most popular musical comedies, *My Fair Lady*, using Shaw's broad outlines, but turning the play from a study in manners to a sentimental love story between pupil and master.

The character of Eliza is best seen by the progression which she makes from "a thing of stone," "a nothingness," a "guttersnipe" and a "squashed cabbage leaf" to the final act where she is an exquisite lady—totally self-possessed, a person who has in many ways surpassed her creator. In the opening act, the audience cannot know that beneath the mud and behind the horrible speech sounds stands the potential of a great "work of art." This carries through the Pygmalion-Galatea theme in which a crude piece of marble is transformed into a beautiful statue. It is not until the third act, when Eliza makes her appearance at Mrs. Higgins' house, that we know that Eliza possesses a great deal of native intelligence, that she has a perfect ear for all sorts of sounds, an excellent ability at reproducing sounds, a superb memory, and a passionate desire to improve herself.

In the first act, Shaw takes great pains to hide all of Eliza's basic qualities. He shows her not only as a person who completely violates the English language, but, more important, he shows her as a low, vulgar creature – totally without manners. We see her initially as a low-class flower girl who vulgarly tries to solicit money from a well-dressed gentleman, Colonel Pickering, and then as a young girl who is vulgarly familiar to another gentleman (Freddy Eynsford-Hill, who ironically wants her to be familiar with him when she becomes a lady); last, we see her as a person who is obnoxious in her protestations, when she thinks that she is about to be accused of prostitution. Thus, what Shaw has done is to let us listen to a flower girl who totally violates the English language and who is a total vulgarian in terms of language. The change in Eliza's pronunciation will come about because of Higgins' lessons in phonetics; but the important change, and the real subject of the play, is the change that will come about in Eliza's manners – something which even Higgins cannot teach her because he has no manners himself.

Eliza arrives at Higgins' laboratory-living room for rather ironic reasons. She wants to adopt middle-class manners that both Higgins and her father despise. Eliza's ideal is to become a member of the respectable middle class, and in order to do so, she must learn proper pronunciation and manners. But then we notice that in spite of the original motive, Eliza's monumental efforts to master her lessons have their bases in the fact that she has developed a "dog-like" devotion to her two masters – a devotion which Higgins will ultimately reject and which Eliza will ultimately declare herself independent of in the next stage of her development.

In both Acts IV and V, Eliza is seen as a completely transformed person, outwardly. She is poised, dignified, in control of her once spitfire temper, and she has rejected all of the old common vulgarity of her past life. She is no longer willing to be Higgins' creation; she now asserts her own independence. But it is an independence which demands values from life which Higgins cannot give her. Unlike Higgins, who wants to change the world, Eliza wants only to change herself. Unlike Higgins, who can and does stand apart from the common aspects of life, Eliza can be content with Freddy, who simply needs and wants her as a compassionate human being. And whereas Higgins can get along without anyone, Eliza and Freddy need each other. In contrast, Higgins will continue to try to improve the world, while Eliza will make a comfortable home for herself and Freddy.

Alfred Doolittle

Doolittle is not so much a character as he is a vehicle which Shaw manipulates for his own dramatic purposes. Through Doolittle, Shaw is able to make many satirical thrusts at middle-class morality and to make additional comments on class distinctions and on class manners. (It is especially witty when Eliza points out to Higgins that the Professor's so-called equality in the way he treats people shows that he has the same manners as her father because Doolittle makes no class distinctions either: the analogy wounds Higgins because he has to acknowledge that it is essentially true.)

As his name readily suggests, Doolittle does as little as possible to get through life. He is a dustman because that is easier for him than "real work." (A dustman was a person who simply collected the ashes that people put out; by Shaw's time, refuse was added to the ashes, making Doolittle essentially a garbage collector.)

The comedy connected with Doolittle is his transformation during the course of the play. Whereas his daughter wants to become a member of the respectable middle class, Doolittle is delighted that his job as dustman is so low on the social class scale that it has absolutely no morals connected to it; therefore, he is not subjected to "dreadful" middle-class morality – at least not until the last act.

When we first meet Doolittle, he comes to Professor Higgins' house in the hypocritical role of the "virtuous father" in order to rescue his "compromised daughter." It is soon discovered, however, that he threw his daughter out into the streets to earn her own living over two years ago, and, furthermore, he was never married to

Eliza's mother. In fact, the people in the neighborhood won't even let Doolittle have any of Eliza's belongings. When the ruse of the virtuous father fails, Doolittle quickly changes his pitch and becomes the ingratiating pimp as he tries to sell his own daughter to the men for almost any price they are willing to pay. Higgins and Pickering are not taken in by his nauseating suggestions, however, but they are delighted by Doolittle's poetic use of the English language, by his use of rhetoric that could only be used by a Welshman, and by his ingenuity as he tries one method after another until he assumes a philosophical pose; in his resourceful rhetoric, he stoutly proclaims that too much charity has been directed at the "deserving poor." Now is it time for him to claim his equal share as a member of the "undeserving poor." An undeserving poor man, according to Doolittle, has as much right to go on a drunken binge as does a deserving poor man; furthermore, if they will give him some money, he will promise to spend it all on a drunken binge immediately and will thus be broke and ready for work on Monday morning.

The originality of this idea, and the audacity and impudence with which it is put forward, cause Higgins and Pickering to yield to Doolittle's request, and they even offer him ten pounds, but Doolittle refuses because it would involve him in responsibilities; he can't drink up ten pounds in the weekend, but he can drink up five pounds.

In the last act, Doolittle's character does not essentially change. It is only that through a large sum of money, he has been forced to accept responsibilities that he would rather not have been faced with. The immoral blackmailer and pimp of the second act has now been forced into the role of a lecturer on moral reforms, and he must now adopt middle-class morality. Since Shaw philosophically wanted to do completely away with the lower class, he is pleased to force Doolittle into accepting a position where he will not be comfortable being one of the "undeserving poor"; Shaw undoubtedly was secretly delighted at the discomfiture that Doolittle was undergoing.

QUESTIONS FOR REVIEW

1.   What is the dramatic importance of phonetics in all of the acts?

2. How is phonetics related to manners in all of the acts?

3. What is the dramatic function of the Eynsford-Hill family in the first act?

4. How might Alfred Doolittle be considered extraneous to the play? How would the play be different if his part were left out of a production?

5. How does Doolittle's change in social position reflect on Eliza's transformation?

6. How are Mrs. Pearce and Mrs. Higgins more alike than is Eliza to each of these ladies? How is she similar to each of them?

7. Discuss the relationship between Higgins and his mother.

8. Explain the numerous intentional violations of manners on Higgins' part. At the end of the play, how can we tolerate the fact that Higgins calls Eliza a "damned impudent slut"?

9. Who should be given the most credit for Eliza's transformation from a flower girl into a duchess? Could either Eliza or Higgins have accomplished this feat without the other?

10. Why do you think that Higgins and Eliza should never marry? Or do you think that they should marry? Explain.

ARMS AND THE MAN

INTRODUCTION

One of Shaw's aims in this play is to debunk the romantic heroics of war; he wanted to present a realistic account of war and to remove all pretensions of nobility from war. It is *not*, however, an anti-war play; instead, it is a satire on those attitudes which would glorify war. To create this satire, Shaw chose as his title the opening lines of Virgil's *Aeneid*, the Roman epic which glorifies war and the heroic feats of man in war, and which begins, "Of arms and the man I sing. . . ."

When the play opens, we hear about the glorious exploits which were performed by Major Sergius Saranoff during his daring and magnificent cavalry raid, an event that turned the war against the Serbs toward victory for the Bulgarians. He thus becomes Raina Petkoff's ideal hero; yet the more that we learn about this raid, the more we realize that it was a futile, ridiculous gesture, one that bordered on an utter suicidal escapade.

In contrast, Captain Bluntschli's actions in Raina's bedroom strikes us, at first, as being the actions of a coward. (Bluntschli is a Swiss, a professional soldier fighting for the Serbs.) He climbs up a waterpipe and onto a balcony to escape capture, he threatens a defenseless woman with his gun, he allows her to hide him behind the curtains, and then he reveals that he carries chocolates rather than cartridges in his cartridge box because chocolates are more practical on the battlefield. Yet, as the play progresses, Bluntschli's unheroic actions become reasonable when we see that he survives, whereas had the war continued, Sergius' absurd heroic exploits would soon have left him dead.

Throughout the play, Shaw arranged his material so as to satirize the glories associated with war and to ultimately suggest that aristocratic pretensions have no place in today's wars, which are won by using business-like efficiency, such as the practical matters of which Bluntschli is a master. For example, Bluntschli is able to deal with the business of dispensing an army to another town with ease, while this was a feat that left the aristocrats (Majors Petkoff and Saranoff) completely baffled. This early play by Shaw, therefore, cuts through the noble ideals of war and the "higher love" that Raina and Sergius claim to share; *Arms and the Man* presents a world where the practical man who lives with no illusions and no poetic views about either love or war is shown to be the superior creature.

LIST OF CHARACTERS

Captain Bluntschli

A professional soldier from Switzerland who is serving in the Serbian army. He is thirty-four years old, and he is totally realistic about the stupidity of war.

Raina Petkoff

The romantic idealist of twenty-three who views war in terms of noble and heroic deeds.

Sergius Saranoff

The extremely handsome young Bulgarian officer who leads an attack against the Serbs which was an overwhelming success.

Major Petkoff

The inept, fifty-year-old father of Raina; he is wealthy by Bulgarian standards, but he is also unread, uncouth, and incompetent.

Catherine Petkoff

Raina's mother; she looks like and acts like a peasant, but she wears fashionable dressing gowns and tea gowns all the time in an effort to appear to be a Viennese lady.

Louka

The Petkoffs' female servant; she is young and physically attractive, and she uses her appearance for ambitious preferment.

Nicola

A realistic, middle-aged servant who is very practical.

GENERAL PLOT SUMMARY

The play begins in the bedroom of Raina Petkoff in a Bulgarian town in 1885, during the Serbo-Bulgarian War. As the play opens, Catherine Petkoff and her daughter, Raina, have just heard that the Bulgarians have scored a tremendous victory in a cavalry charge led by Raina's fiancé, Major Sergius Saranoff, who is in the same regiment as Raina's father, Major Paul Petkoff. Raina is so impressed with the noble deeds of her fiancé that she fears that she might never be able to live up to his nobility. At this very moment, the maid, Louka, rushes in with the news that the Serbs are being chased through the streets and that it is necessary to lock up the house and all of the windows. Raina promises to do so later, and Louka leaves. But as Raina is reading in bed, shots are heard, there is a noise at the balcony window, and a bedraggled enemy soldier with a gun appears and threatens to kill her if she makes a sound. After the soldier and Raina exchange some words, Louka calls from outside the door; she says that several soldiers want to search the house and investigate a report that an enemy Serbian soldier was seen climbing her balcony. When Raina hears the news, she turns to the soldier. He says that he is prepared to die, but he certainly plans to kill a few Bulgarian soldiers in her bedroom before he dies. Thus, Raina impetuously decides to hide him. The soldiers investigate, find no one, and leave. Raina then calls the man out from hiding; she nervously and absentmindedly sits on his gun, but she learns that it is not loaded; the soldier carries no cartridges. He explains that instead of carrying bullets, he always carries chocolates into battle. Furthermore, he is not an enemy; he is a Swiss, a professional soldier hired by Serbia. Raina gives him the last of her chocolate creams, which he devours, maintaining that she has indeed saved his life. Now that the Bulgarian soldiers are gone, Raina wants the "chocolate cream soldier" (as she calls him) to climb back down the drainpipe, but he refuses to; whereas he could climb *up*, he hasn't the strength to climb down. When Raina goes after her mother to help, the "chocolate cream soldier" crawls into Raina's bed and falls instantly asleep. In fact, when they re-enter, he is sleeping so soundly that they cannot awaken him.

Act II begins four months later in the garden of Major Petkoff's house. The middle-aged servant Nicola is lecturing Louka on the importance of having proper respect for the upper class, but Louka has too independent a soul to ever be a "proper" servant. She has higher plans for herself than to marry someone like Nicola, who, she insists, has the "soul of a servant." Major Petkoff arrives home from the war, and his wife Catherine greets him with two bits of information: she suggests that Bulgaria should have annexed Serbia, and she tells him that she has had an electric bell installed in the library. Major Sergius Saranoff, Raina's fiancé and leader of the successful cavalry charge, arrives, and in the course of discussing the end of the war, he and Major Petkoff recount the now-famous story of how a Swiss soldier escaped by climbing up a balcony and into the bedroom of a noble Bulgarian woman. The women are shocked that such a crude story would be told in front of them. When the Petkoffs go into the house, Raina and Sergius discuss their love for one another, and Raina romantically declares that the two of them have found a "higher love."

When Raina goes to get her hat so that they can go for a walk, Louka comes in, and Sergius asks if she knows how tiring it is to be involved with a "higher love." Then he immediately tries to embrace the attractive maid. Since he is being so blatantly familiar, Louka declares that Miss Raina is no better than she; Raina, she says, has been having an affair while Sergius was away, but she refuses to tell Sergius who Raina's lover is, even though Sergius accidently bruises Louka's arm while trying to wrest a confession from her. When he apologizes, Louka insists that he kiss her arm, but Sergius refuses and, at that moment, Raina re-enters. Sergius is then called away, and Catherine enters. The two ladies discuss how incensed they both are that Sergius related the tale about the escaping soldier. Raina, however, doesn't care if Sergius hears about it; she is tired of his stiff propriety. At that moment, Louka announces the presence of a Swiss officer with a carpetbag, calling for the lady of the house. His name is Captain Bluntschli. Instantly, they both know he is the "chocolate cream soldier" who is returning the Major's old coat that they disguised him in. As they make rapid, desperate plans to send him away, Major Petkoff hails Bluntschli and greets him warmly as the person who aided them in the final negotiations of the war; the old Major insists that Bluntschli must their houseguest until he has to return to Switzerland.

Act III begins shortly after lunch and takes place in the library. Captain Bluntschli is attending to a large amount of confusing paperwork in a very efficient manner, while Sergius and Major Petkoff merely observe. Major Petkoff complains about a favorite old coat being lost, but at that moment Catherine rings the new library bell, sends Nicola after the coat, and astounds the Major by thus retrieving his lost coat. When Raina and Bluntschli are left alone, she compliments him on his looking so handsome now that he is washed and brushed. Then she assumes a high and noble tone and chides him concerning certain stories which he has told and the fact that she has had to lie for him. Bluntschli laughs at her "noble attitude" and says that he is pleased with her demeanor. Raina is amused; she says that Bluntschli is the first person to ever see through her pretensions, but she is perplexed that he didn't feel into the pockets of the old coat which she lent him; she had placed a photo of herself there with the inscription "To my Chocolate Cream Soldier." At this moment, a telegram is brought to Bluntschli, relating the death of his father and the necessity of his coming home immediately to make arrangements for the six hotels that he has inherited. As Raina and Bluntschli leave the room, Louka comes in wearing her sleeve in a ridiculous fashion so that her bruise will be obvious. Sergius enters and asks if he can cure it now with a kiss. Louka questions his true bravery; she wonders if he has the courage to marry a woman who is socially beneath him, even if he loved the woman. Sergius asserts that he would, but he is now engaged to a girl so noble that all such talk is absurd. Louka then lets him know that Bluntschli is his rival and that Raina will marry the Swiss soldier. Sergius is incensed. He sees Bluntschli and immediately challenges him to a duel; then he retracts when Raina comes in and accuses him of making love to Louka merely to spy on her and Bluntschli. As they are arguing, Bluntschli asks for Louka, who has been eavesdropping at the door. She is brought in, Sergius apologizes to her, kisses her hand, and thus they become engaged. Bluntschli asks permission to become a suitor for Raina's hand, and when

54

he lists all of the possessions which he has (200 horses, 9600 pairs of sheets, ten thousand knives and forks, etc.), permission for the marriage is granted, and Bluntschli says that he will return in two weeks to marry Raina. Succumbing with pleasure, Raina gives a loving smile to her "chocolate cream soldier."

PREFACE

Unlike *Pygmalion* or many other of Shaw's plays, there is no actual, separate preface to *this* particular play. However, there was a preface to the original volume of plays which contains this play and three others: *The Pleasant Plays*, 1898, revised in 1921. As Shaw noted elsewhere, a preface seldom or never concerns the play which is to follow the preface, and this preface is no exception. Instead, Shaw used this preface to comment upon the new style of drama (or simply what he calls New Drama), a name applied to dramas such as his or Ibsen's, plays which were not written to be commercial successes, but to be intellectual vehicles which would make the audience consider (or think about) their life – to be intellectually aware of their historical place in civilization. Shaw refuses to pander himself to popular demands for romantic (and thus unbelievable and unrealistic) situations. Ultimately, according to Shaw, the theater should become a place for the airing of ideas and a place where sham and pretense can be exposed in a way that is delightful to the audience.

SUMMARIES AND COMMENTARIES

ACT I

Summary

The play opens at night in a lady's bedchamber in a small Bulgarian town in 1885, the year of the Serbo-Bulgarian war. The room is decorated in the worst possible taste, a taste reflected in the mistress' (Catherine Petkoff's) desire to seem as cultured and as Viennese as possible. But the room is furnished with only cheap bits of Viennese things; the other pieces of furniture come from the

Turkish Ottoman Empire, reflecting the long occupation by the Turks of the Balkan peninsula. On the balcony, standing and staring at the romantic beauty of the night, "intensely conscious that her own youth and beauty are a part of it," is young Raina Petkoff. Just inside, conspicuously visible, is a box of chocolate creams, which will play an important part later in this act and which will ultimately become a symbol of the type of war which Shaw will satirize.

Raina's mother, Catherine Petkoff, is a woman who could easily pass for a splendid specimen of the wife of a mountain farmer, but is determined to be a Viennese lady. As the play begins, Catherine is excited over the news that the Bulgarian forces have just won a splendid battle at Slivnitza against the Serbians, and the "hero of the hour, the idol of the regiment" who led them to victory is Raina's fiancé, Sergius Saranoff. She describes how Sergius boldly led a cavalry charge into the midst of the Serbs, scattering them in all directions. Raina wonders if such a popular hero will care any longer for her little affections, but she is nonetheless delighted about the news. She wonders if heroes such as Sergius esteem such heroic ideas because they have read too much Byron and Pushkin. Real life, as she knows, is quite different.

They are interrupted by the entry of Louka, a handsome and proud peasant girl, who announces that the Serbs have been routed, have scattered throughout the town, and that some of the fugitives have been chased into the neighborhood. Thus, the doors must be secured since there might be fighting and shooting in the street below. Raina is annoyed that the fugitives must be killed, but she is immediately corrected – in war, *everyone* can be killed. Catherine goes below to fasten up the doors, and Louka shows Raina how to fasten the shutters if there is any shooting; then she leaves to help bolt the rest of the house.

Left alone, Raina picks up her fiancé's picture, raises it above her head like a priestess worshipping it, and calls the portrait her "soul's hero." As she prepares for bed, shots are suddenly heard in the distance and then some more shots are heard; these are much nearer. She scrambles out of bed, rapidly blows out the candles, and immediately darts back into bed. She hears more shots, then she hears someone tampering with the shutters from outside; there is a glimmer of light, and then someone strikes a match and warns her not to try to run away. Raina is told to light a candle, and after she does so, she is able to see a man in a Serbian's officer's uniform; he is completely bespattered with mud and blood, and he warns her that if it becomes necessary, he will shoot her because if he is caught, he will be killed—and he has no intention of dying. When they hear a disturbance outside the house, the Serbian officer quickly snatches Raina's cloak that she is about to use to cover herself; ungentlemanlike, he keeps it, knowing that she won't want a group of army officers searching her room when she is clad in only a sheer nightgown. There is more noise downstairs, and Louka is heard at the door; she says that there is a search party downstairs, and if Raina doesn't let them in, they will break down the door. Suddenly the Serbian officer loses his courage; he tells Raina that he is done for. He will shoot the first man who breaks in and "it will not be nice." Raina impulsively changes her mind and decides to hide him behind the curtains. Catherine, Louka, and a Russian officer dressed in a Bulgarian uniform enter, and after inspecting the balcony and hearing Raina testify that no one came in, they leave. (Louka, however, notices something behind the curtain and sees the revolver lying on the ottoman; she says nothing, however.) Raina slams and locks the door after them.

When the Serbian officer emerges and offers his thanks, he explains that he is not really a Serbian officer; he is a professional soldier, a Swiss citizen, in fact, and he now wishes that he had joined with the Bulgarians rather than with the Serbs. He asks to stay a minute to collect his thoughts, and Raina agrees, deciding to sit down also, but as she sits on the ottoman, she sits on the man's pistol, and she lets out a scream. Raina now realizes what it was that Louka was staring at, and she is surprised that the others didn't notice it. She is frightened of the gun, but the soldier tells her there is no need to be—it is not loaded: he keeps chocolates rather than bullets in his cartridge holder. In fact, he wishes he had some chocolates now. In mock scorn, Raina goes to the chest of drawers and returns with a half-eaten box of chocolates, the remainder of which he immediately devours. Raina is shocked to hear him say that only foolish young soldiers or else stupid ones like those in charge of the recent attack on the Serbs at Slivnitza carry bullets; wise and experienced soldiers carry chocolates. Then he offends her further (and still innocently, of course,) by explaining how unprofessional the cavalry charge against the Serbians was, and if there had not been a stupid mistake on the part of the Serbs, the Bulgarians would have been massacred. Then the soldier says that the Bulgarian "hero," the leader of the troops, acted "like an operatic tenor . . . shouting his war-cry and charging like Don Quixote at the windmills." He says that the fellow was the laughing stock of everyone present: "Of all the fools let loose on a field of battle, that man must be the very maddest." Only a stupid mistake carried the day for him. Raina then takes the portrait of Sergius and shows it to the officer, who agrees that this was indeed the person who was "charging the windmills and imagining he was doing the finest thing."

Angry at the derogatory remarks about her "heroic" betrothed, Raina orders the stranger to leave. But he balks; he says that whereas he could climb *up* the balcony, he simply can't face the descent. He is so exhausted that he tells her to simply give out the alarm—he's beaten. Raina tries to spark some courage in him, but realizes that he is more prudent than daring. Raina is at a loss; she simply doesn't know what to do with him: he can't be caught in the Petkoff house, the richest house in Bulgaria and the only one to have a library and an inside staircase. She then remembers an opera by Verdi, *Ernani*, in which a fugitive throws himself on the mercy of some aristocratic people; she thinks that perhaps this might be the solution because, according to the opera, the hospitality of a nobleman is sacred and inviolable. In response, the soldier tells her that his father is a hospitable man himself; in fact, he owns six hotels in Switzerland. Then falling asleep, he kisses her hand. Raina panics. She insists that he stay awake until she can fetch her mother, but before she can get out of the room, he has crawled into her bed and is asleep in such a trance that when Raina returns with her mother, they cannot shake him awake. His fatigue is so great that Raina tells her mother: "The poor darling is worn out. Let him sleep." This comment arouses Catherine's stern reproach, and the curtain falls on the first act.

Commentary

In reading a Shavian play, one should pay attention to Shaw's staging directions at the beginning of the act. The stage directions here call for the scenery to convey the impression of cheap Viennese pretentious aristocracy incongruously combined with good, solid Bulgarian commonplace items. Likewise, since Raina will ultimately be seen as a person who will often assume a pose for dramatic effect, the act opens with her being (in Shaw's words) "intensely conscious of the romantic beauty of the night and of the fact that her own youth and beauty are part of it." As we find out later, she even listens at doors and waits until the proper moment to make the most effective, dramatic entrance.

As noted in the "Introduction" to these notes, the title of this play is ironic since it comes from the opening line of Virgil's *Aeneid* ("Of arms and the man I sing. . . ."), an epic which glorifies war and the hero in battle. Shaw will use the idea of the hero (Sergius) in war (the Serbo-Bulgarian war) in order to satirize not merely war itself, but the romantic glorification of war. In addition to this goal, he will also satirize romantic notions of valor and courage, affectation and pretense, and most important, misguided idealism. The dramatic shift that will occur in the play involves two romantic idealists (Raina and Sergius) who, rejecting their original positions instead of marrying each other, will each become engaged to a practical realist – Sergius to the practical and attractive servant, Louka, and Raina to the professional realist, Captain Bluntschli.

Raina is seen, at first, as the romantic idealist, but she is also characterized as being a fleeting realist when she wonders if her idealism and Sergius' idealism might be due simply to the fact that they have read so much poetry by Byron and other romantics. Likewise, Raina wants to glory in the noble idealism of the war, but she is also deeply troubled by its cruelty: "What glory is there in killing wretched fugitives?" In this early comment, we have her rationale for her later hiding and, thus, her saving Bluntschli's life.

Before meeting Bluntschli, Raina seems to want to live according to the romantic idealism to which she and Sergius aspire. She knows that he has, in effect, placed her on too high a pedestal, but she does want to make an effort to live "up to his high standards." For example, after hearing of his heroic feats, she holds up his photo and "elevates it, like a preistess," vowing never to be unworthy of him. This vow, however, as we soon see, will not last too long.

Captain Bluntschli's arrival through the balcony doors is, in itself, a highly melodramatic and romantic stage entrance. In fact, almost everything about Act I is contrived – the lady's bedroom, the concealment of the fugitive behind a curtain, the threat of a bloody fight, the matter of chocolate creams, and, finally, the enemy soldier falling asleep in the lady's bed – all of this smacks of artificiality and is juxtaposed against Captain Bluntschli's realistic appraisal of war and his matter-of-fact assertion that, from a practical viewpoint, Sergius' military charge was as foolish as Don Quixote's charge on the Windmills. And actually, while Raina ridicules Captain Blunt-schli for his cowardice, for his hiding behind a woman's curtains, for his inordinate fear (he has been under fire for three days and his nerves are "shot to pieces"), and for his extraordinary desire for chocolate creams, she is nevertheless attracted to him, and even though she pretends to be offended at his comments about Sergius, she is secretly happy that her fiancé is not as perfect as we were earlier led to believe that he was.

At the end of the act, Raina returns to her artificial pretensions as she tries to impress Bluntschli with her family's aristocratic aspirations, bragging that her father chose the only house in the city with an inside stairway, and a library, and, furthermore, Raina says, she attends the opera every year in Bucharest. Ironically, it is from romantic operas that Raina derives many of her romantic ideals, and she uses one of Verdi's romantic operas as her rationale for hiding this practical Swiss professional soldier. The final irony of the act is that the professional man of war is sleeping as soundly as a baby in Raina's bed, with her hovering over him, feeling protective about him.

ACT II

Summary

Some four months have passed since the first act, and a peace treaty has just been signed. The setting for this act is in Major Petkoff's garden. Louka is standing onstage in a disrespectful attitude, smoking a cigarette and talking to Nicola, a middle-aged servant who has "the complacency of the servant who values himself on his rank in servitude." The opening dialogue informs us that Nicola is engaged to Louka, but that he has reservations about her deportment. He refuses to marry a person who is "disrespectful" to her superiors; he plans to open a shop in Sofia, and he thinks that the success of the shop will depend on the goodwill of his employees, and he knows that if they spread bad reports about him, his shop will never be successful. When Louka maintains that she knows secret things about the mistress and the master, Nicola reminds her that *all* servants know secrets about their employers, but the secret of being a good servant is to keep these things secret and to always be discreet; if servants begin telling secrets, then no one will ever employ them again. Louka is furious and says that Nicola has "the soul of a servant"; Nicola agrees — "That is," he says, "the secret of success in service."

Their discussion is interrupted by the entrance of Major Petkoff, an "insignificant, unpolished man," who has just returned from the war. He sends Louka into the house to get his wife and to also bring him some coffee. Catherine comes out and welcomes her husband, and he tells her that the war is over, the peace treaty is signed, and all is now peaceful. When he inquires about his wife's health, she tells him that she has a sore throat. The Major maintains that the soreness comes "from washing [her] neck every day." He himself does not believe in these silly modern notions of washing: "It can't be good for the health; it's not natural. There was an English-man at Philippopolis who used to wet himself all over with cold water every morning when he got up." He maintains that the English climate is so dirty that the English *have* to wash, but others don't; his father, for example, lived to be ninety-eight years old and never had a bath in his entire life.

As Catherine is explaining to her husband about the installation of an electric bell in the library, the Major is confused over its use because — in his opinion — if he wants someone, he will shout for them. At this time, Major Sergius Saranoff arrives; he is "a tall romantically handsome man" and is the original of the portrait in Raina's room in the first act. He is roundly congratulated for his famous charge against the Serbs. Sergius, however, does not appreciate the compliment, because even though he was successful, he participated in a maneuver where the Russian consultants failed; thus, he did not accomplish his great success by the rule book. "Two Cossack colonels had their regiments routed on the most correct principles of scientific warfare. [Furthermore,] Two major-generals got killed strictly according to military etiquette," and now the two colonels who failed are promoted to generals and he (Sergius) who succeeded is still a major; therefore, he has resigned.

As Catherine is protesting that Sergius should not resign – the women, she says, are for him – Sergius suddenly asks, "Where is Raina?" At that very moment, Raina enters sweepingly, announcing, "Raina is here." Sergius drops chivalrously on one knee to kiss her hand. While Raina's father is impressed with the fact that Raina "always appears at the right moment," her mother is annoyed because she knows that Raina always listens at doorways in order to make her entrance at exactly the right moment. Catherine pronounces it to be "an abominable habit."

Raina then welcomes her father home, and again they discuss Sergius' military career. Sergius now views war in a very cynical manner; according to him, there is nothing heroic nor romantic about it. "Soldiering is the coward's art of attacking mercilessly when you are strong, and keeping out of harm's way when you are weak. . . . Never fight [your enemy] on equal terms." Furthermore, he now views soldiering as having too much of the taint of being a trade business, and he *despises* trade; this is, of course, an allusion to Captain Blutschli, who, of course, is in trade, and it is also a reference to Louka's fiancé, Nicola, who wants to go into trade. To prove his point, Sergius asks them all to consider the case of the Swiss officer (Bluntschli) who was able to deal very shrewdly and to make clever bargains concerning prisoners. As a result, soldiering has been "reduced to a matter of trading and bartering." He adds that the man was merely "a commercial traveler in uniform."

Since the subject has come up, Major Petkoff encourages Sergius to tell the story about the Swiss officer who climbed into a Bulgarian lady's bedroom in order to escape capture. Raina, recognizing herself as the woman of the story, pretends to be offended. Major Petkoff therefore tries to get Sergius to help him with some army details, and Catherine instructs Sergius to remain with Raina while Catherine discusses some business with her husband. By this ruse, she is able to leave the two young people alone.

Alone together, Raina looks upon Sergius with admiration and worship: "My hero! My king!" – to which he responds "My queen!" Raina sees Sergius only in terms of the knight of olden times who goes forth to fight heroically, guided only by his lady's love. She believes that the two of them have truly found what she calls the perfect "higher love." When Louka is heard entering the house, Raina leaves to get her hat so that they can go for a walk and be alone. In Louka's presence, Sergius swaggers a bit, then asks Louka if she knows what "higher love" is. Whatever it is, he says, he finds it "fatiguing" to keep it up: "one feels the need of some relief after it." He then embraces Louka, who warns him to be careful; or, at least, if he won't let her go, he should step back where they cannot be seen. After she makes a sly comment about the possibility of Raina's spying on them, Sergius defends Raina and their "higher love," and Louka maintains that she will never understand "gentlefolk" because while Sergius is professing love for Raina, he is flirting with her behind Raina's back, and, furthermore, Raina is doing the same thing. Sergius tries to reprimand Louka for gossiping so about her mistress, but he is visibly upset and dramatically strikes his forehead. He insists that Louka tell him who his rival is, but she will not do so, especially since he has just reprimanded her for talking about her mistress. She tells him that she never actually saw the man; she only heard his voice outside Miss Raina's bedroom. But she knows that if the man ever comes here again, that Raina will marry him. Sergius is furious, and he grips her so tightly that he bruises her arm; he reminds her that because of her gossiping, she has the "soul of a servant," the same accusation which she made earlier about Nicola. Louka retaliates by pointing out that Sergius himself is a liar, and, furthermore, she maintains that she is worth "six of her [Raina]." As Louka begins to leave, Sergius wants to apologize for hurting a woman, no matter what the status of that woman is, but Louka will not accept an apology; she wants more. When Sergius wants to pay her for the injury, Louka says that she wants him to kiss her bruised arm. Surprised, Sergius refuses, and Louka majestically picks up the serving pieces and leaves, just as Raina enters, dressed in the latest fashion of Vienna – of the previous year. Immediately, Catherine calls down that her husband needs Sergius for a few minutes to discuss a business matter.

When Sergius is gone, Catherine enters, and she and Raina express their irritation that "that Swiss" told the entire story of his night in Raina's bedroom. Raina maintains that if she had him here now she would "cram him with chocolate creams." Catherine is frightened that if Sergius finds out the truth about what happened, the engagement will be broken off. Suddenly, however, Raina reveals that she would not care, and that, furthermore, she has always wanted to say something dreadful so as to shock Sergius' propriety, "to scandalize the five senses out of him." She half-hopes that he will find out about her "chocolate cream soldier." She then leaves her mother in a state of shock.

Louka enters and announces the presence of a Serbian soldier at the door, a soldier who is asking for the *lady* of the house; he has sent his card bearing his name—"Captain Bluntschli," thus giving us for the first time the name of the "chocolate cream soldier." When Catherine reads the name and hears that the caller is Swiss, she realizes that he is the "chocolate cream soldier" and that he is return-ing the old coat of Major Petkoff's which they gave him when he left. Catherine gives Louka strict instructions to make sure that the library door is shut; then Louka is to send in the captain and have Nicola bring the visitor's bag to her. When Louka returns with the captain, Catherine frantically explains that her husband and future son-in-law are here and that he must leave immediately. Captain Bluntschli agrees reluctantly and explains that he only wants to take the coat out of his bag, but Catherine urges him to leave it; she will have his bag sent to him later. As Bluntschli is writing out his address, Major Petkoff comes in and greets the captain warmly and enthusiastically. Immediately, Major Petkoff tells the captain that they are in desperate need of help in working out the details of send-ing troops and horses to Philippopolis. Captain Bluntschli im-mediately pinpoints the problem, and as they are about to go into the library to explain the details, Raina enters and bumps into the captain and surprisedly exclaims loudly: "Oh! the chocolate cream soldier." She immediately regains her composure and explains that she was cooking a kind of dessert and had made a chocolate cream soldier for its decoration and that Nicola sat a pile of plates on it. At that moment, Nicola brings in the captain's bag, saying that Catherine told him to do so; when Catherine denies it, Major Petkoff thinks that Nicola must be losing his mind. He reprimands Nicola (for doing what Nicola has been commanded to do), and at this point Nicola is so confused that he drops the bag, almost hitting the Ma-jor's foot. As the women try to placate the Major, he, in turn, urges Captain Bluntschli to remain as their houseguest until he has to return to Switzerland. Even though Catherine has been subtly suggesting that Captain Bluntschli leave, Bluntschli agrees to remain.

Commentary

Arms and the Man is an early Shavian play, and in it, Shaw used certain techniques that he was never to use again. In the first act, for example, the entire act has a farcical note about it and the use of a screen or a curtain for a character to hide behind was a traditional technique used only in comedies. The coat episode in the third act is a contrived bit of farce that amuses the audience, but it cheapens the intellectual aspect of the drama because it contributes nothing other than its own farcical element.

In Act II, the structure of the act is more serious, but it also uses several traditional farcical elements. For example, there is the use of the exaggerated means whereby Sergius can deceive Raina while trying to make love with Raina's maid, the story told in the army camp about the soldier who escapes into a lady's bedroom (while the ladies of the story have to listen in pretended dismay), and there is the sudden appearance of the captain and the hasty decisions which the ladies must undertake, and finally there is the sudden surprise that occurs when we discover that Captain Petkoff knows Bluntschli — all of these circumstances are elements of melodrama or farce.

In the early part of the act, we see Louka as an ingenious maid who refuses to acknowledge that she has "the soul of a servant," a fault that she accuses Nicola of having. Later, however, when Sergius tells her that *she* possesses the soul of a servant, his comment stings. We do, however, admire the way that Louka is able to dismiss Nicola and to manipulate the supposedly superior and aristocratic Sergius.

When we meet Sergius and hear of his total disillusionment with war and with "soldiering [which] is the coward's art of attacking mercilessly when you are strong and keeping out of the way when you are weak," we are then prepared for the fact that Sergius will not be a romantic idealist for long. His new views on war should prepare us for a significant change in his total outlook on life; thus, he will soon reject Raina's idealistic "higher love" in favor of a more direct love with the attractive and practical Louka, a maid who says forthrightly that if Sergius is going to embrace her, then at least they should stand back where they can't be seen. With Louka, Sergius can admit that there are at least six different people occupying himself – and then wonder aloud, "Which of the six is the real man? That's the question that torments me." We now know that the real Sergius is *not* the one with whom Raina has fallen in love, the one with the "higher love." Thus, by the end of this act, Shaw has set up all of the necessary motives and reasons for Sergius and Raina to break off their engagement and marry someone else.

ACT III

Summary

This act shifts to the Petkoffs' library, a setting which Shaw uses to let us know that this is a very poor excuse for a library; it consists of only a single room, with a single shelf of old worn-out paper-covered novels; the rest of the room is more like a sitting room, with another ottoman in it, just like the one in Raina's room in the first act. The room is also fitted with an old kitchen table which serves as a writing table. At the opening of the act, Bluntschli is busy at work preparing orders, with a businesslike regularity, for the disposition of the Bulgarian army. Petkoff is more of a hinderance than a help, for he constantly interrupts to see if he can be of any help. Finally, his wife tells him to stop interrupting. Petkoff, in turn, complains that all that he needs to be comfortable is his favorite old coat, which he can't find. Catherine rings for Nicola and tells the servant to go to the blue closet and fetch his master's old coat. Petkoff is so certain that it is not there that he is willing to make a bet of an expensive piece of jewelry with her. Sergius is about to enter a bet also, but Nicola suddenly returns with the coat. Petkoff is completely astonished and perplexed when Nicola announces that it was indeed hanging in the *blue* closet.

At this moment, Bluntschli finishes the last order, gives it to Sergius to take to his soldiers, and then asks Petkoff to follow to make sure that Sergius doesn't make a mistake. Petkoff asks his wife to come along because she is good at giving commands. Left alone with Raina, Bluntschli expresses his astonishment at an army where "officers send for their wives to keep discipline."

Raina then tells Captain Bluntschli how much better he looks now that he is clean, and she inquires about his experiences after he left her bedroom. She lets him know that the entire story has been told so many times that both her father and her fiancé are aware of the story—but not the identities of the people involved. In fact, Raina believes that "if Sergius knew, he would challenge you and kill you in a duel." Bluntschli says that he hopes that Raina won't tell, but Raina tells him of her desire to be perfectly open and honest with Sergius. Because of Bluntschli, Raina says, she has now told two lies—one to the soldiers looking for him in her room and another one just now about the chocolate pudding—and she feels terrible about lying; Bluntschli cannot take her seriously. In fact, he tells her that when "you strike that noble attitude and speak in that thrilling voice, I admire you; but I find it impossible to believe a single word you say." At first, Raina is indignant, but then she is highly amused that Bluntschli has seen through the disguise that she has used since she was a child: "You know, I've always gone on like that," she tells him.

When Raina asks him what he thought of her for giving him a portrait of herself, Bluntschli tells her that he never received it because he never reached into the pocket of the coat where Raina had put it. He is not concerned until he learns that Raina inscribed upon it "To my Chocolate Cream Soldier." In the meantime, Bluntschli confesses, he pawned the coat thinking that was the safest place for it. Raina is furious, and she accuses him of having a "shopkeeping mind." At this point, they are interrupted by Louka, who brings Bluntschli some letters and telegrams, which inform him that his father has died and that Bluntschli has inherited several hotels which he will have to manage. He must leave immediately. Alarmed, Raina follows him out.

Nicola enters and sees Louka with her sleeve rolled up so as to expose her bruised arm, and he reprimands her. Then they argue over the duties and obligations of being a servant. Louka says that she absolutely refuses to act like a servant, and Nicola answers that he is quite willing to release her from their engagement if she can better herself. Then, he would have another customer for his shop, one who would bring him good business. When Sergius enters, Nicola leaves immediately, and Sergius, noticing the bruise on Louka's arm, asks if he can cure it now by kissing it. Louka reminds him of his place *and* of hers. She wonders aloud if Sergius is a brave man and if poor people are any less brave than wealthy people. Sergius answers that in war any man can have courage: "the courage to rage and [to] kill is cheap." Louka then asks if Sergius has true courage; that is, would he dare to marry someone whom he loved if that person was socially beneath him? She asserts that she thinks that Sergius would "be afraid of what other people would say," and thus he would never have the courage to marry beneath him. Sergius contradicts her until Louka tells him that Raina will never marry him, that Raina is going to marry the Swiss soldier. As she turns to go, Sergius grabs her and holds her firmly; as he threatens her and questions the truth of her accusation, she wonders if anyone would believe the fact that she is now in his arms. He releases her with the assertion that if he ever touches her again, it will be as her fiancé.

As Louka leaves, Bluntschli enters and is immediately told by Sergius where he is to be on the following morning; they will duel on horseback and with sabres. Bluntschli maintains that as the challenged party, it is his privilege to choose the weapons, and he plans to have a machine gun. But when Bluntschli sees that Sergius is serious, he agrees to meet him with a sabre, but he refuses to fight on horseback because it is too dangerous. Raina enters then, in time to hear their last arrangements. Bluntschli explains that he is an expert with the sword and that he will see to it that neither of them are hurt; afterward, he will leave immediately for Switzerland and no one will ever hear of the incident. Sergius then accuses Bluntschli of receiving favors from Raina which he (Sergius) has never enjoyed—that is, she received Bluntschli in her bedroom. Bluntschli points out that she did so "with a pistol at her head. . . . I'd have blown out her brains if she'd uttered a cry." Sergius cannot accept the story that there is nothing between the two because if it were true, then Captain Bluntschli would not have come back to the Petkoff house. He could have sent the coat; he came only to see Raina.

When Sergius makes further accusations, Raina reminds him that she saw him and Louka in each other's arms, and she now understands about their relationship. Sergius realizes that his and Raina's engagement is over, and he therefore cancels the duel with Bluntschli, who is pleased to get out of it since he didn't want to fight in the first place. Raina, however, is furious, and she tells Bluntschli that Sergius had Louka spy on them and that Sergius rewarded Louka by making love to her. As they continue to argue, Bluntschli tries to get Sergius to stop because he is losing the argument. Suddenly, Bluntschli asks where Louka is. Raina maintains that she is listening at the door, and as Sergius stoutly denies such a thing, Raina goes to the door and drags Louka inside; she was, in fact, eavesdropping. Louka is not ashamed; she says that her love is at stake and that her feelings for Sergius are stronger than Raina's feelings for the "chocolate cream soldier."

At this point, Major Petkoff enters in short sleeves; his old coat is being mended. When Nicola enters with it, Raina helps him on with the coat and deftly removes the inscribed portrait from the coat pocket. Thus, when her father reaches for the photograph to ask Raina the meaning of a photograph of her with the inscription: "Raina, to her Chocolate Cream Soldier: A Souvenir," the photo is missing! Major Petkoff is confused and asks Sergius if he is the "chocolate cream soldier." The Major responds indignantly that he is *not*. Then Bluntschli explains that *he* is the "chocolate cream soldier" and that Raina saved his life. Petkoff is further confused when Raina points out that Louka is the true object of Sergius' affections—despite the fact that Louka is engaged to Nicola, who denies this and says that he is hoping for Louka's good recommendation when he opens his shop.

Suddenly Louka feels as though she is being bartered, and she demands an apology; when Sergius kisses her hand in apology, she reminds him that his touch now makes her his "affianced wife," and even though Sergius had forgotten his earlier statement, he still holds true to his word and claims Louka for his own. At this moment, Catherine enters and is shocked to find Louka and Sergius together. Louka explains that Raina is fond only of Bluntschli, and before Raina can answer, Bluntschli explains that such a young and beautiful girl as Raina could not be in love with a thirty-four-year-old soldier who is an incurable romantic; the only reason he came back, he says, was not to return the coat but to get just one more glance at Raina, but he fears that she is no more than seventeen years old. Raina then tells Bluntschli that he is indeed foolishly romantic if he thinks that she, a twenty-three-year-old woman, is a seventeen-year-old-*girl*. At this point, Bluntschli asks permission to be a suitor for Raina's hand. When he is reminded that Sergius comes from an old family which kept at least twenty horses, Bluntschli begins to enumerate all of the possessions (including two hundred horses) which *he* owns; he fails, however, to mention that his possessions are connected with the hotel business that he has just inherited. His list of possessions are so impressive that it is agreed that he shall indeed marry Raina, who is delighted with her "chocolate cream soldier." As Bluntschli leaves, with the promise of being back in two weeks, Sergius looks in wonder and comments "What a man! Is he a man!"

Commentary

After the farcical bit about the discovery of the old coat in the blue closet, which perplexes Major Petkoff, Shaw then gets down to the resolution of the drama, which involves the revealing of Raina's, Sergius', and Bluntschli's true natures.

First, in Bluntschli's interview with Raina, we see him as the practical man who will not let Raina assume any of her poses; he will laugh at all of the poses that she assumes. Captain Bluntschli, while being charmed and captivated by Raina, refuses to take her poses seriously; that is, he delights in her posturing, but he is not deceived by them: "When you strike that noble attitude and speak in that thrilling voice, I admire you; but I find it impossible to believe a single word you say." Thus, Bluntschli forces Raina to reveal her true nature, and she is delighted that someone has seen through her guise and has allowed her to come down off her pedestal. We were earlier prepared for this revelation when she told her mother that she would like to shock Sergius; already, we have seen that she finds "higher love" to be something of a strain on her. Thus, it is ultimately a relief for her to discard all of her artificial poses and finally become herself.

Likewise, Bluntschli changes. While he will not tolerate posturing, yet, since he is such a plainspoken man, we are surprised to discover that beneath his exterior, he has a romantic soul—that is, he came back with the Major's coat only to have one more glimpse of Raina, with whom he is infatuated. Therefore, as the practical man is seen to change, so also does Sergius, whom we saw very early in the second act confess to being tired of playing this game of the ideal of the "higher love." He is immensely relieved not to have to be the over-idealized, noble object of Raina's love; he found it tiresome, trying to live up to her expectations. After discovering that there is no nobility or heroics connected with war, he is delighted to discover that Raina's heroics are not for him; as a result, he turns to the more basic but yet attractive Louka.

The resolution of the drama is brought about by the simple technique of having all of the characters recognize their basic nature and yield to it. Consequently, the ending of this comedy is similar to most classic comedies—that is, after a mix-up or confusion between the lovers, everyone is paired with the proper person finally.

CHARACTER ANALYSES

Raina Petkoff

Raina is one of Shaw's most delightful heroines from his early plays. In the opening scenes of the play, she is presented as being a romantically idealistic person in love with the noble ideal of war and love; yet, she is also aware that she is playing a game, that she is a *poseuse* who enjoys making dramatic entrances (her mother is aware that Raina listens at doors in order to know when to make an effective entrance), and she is very quixotic in her views on love and war.

Whenever Raina strikes a pose, she is fully aware "of the fact that her own youth and beauty are part of it." When she accuses Bluntschli of being "incapable of gratitude" and "incapable of any noble sentiments," she is also amused, and she is later delighted that he sees through her "noble attitude" and her pretensions. In fact, her attraction for Bluntschli is partly due to the fact that she can step down off the pedestal which she must be upon, metaphorically, whenever she is in Sergius' presence. She shocks her mother when she says that she would like to shock Sergius' propriety since he is such a "stuffed shirt." Yet, at first, she is filled with undefined ideals. She admires Sergius' victories, but she is also genuinely troubled by the reports of the suffering and slaughter that accompany the war. She does respond immediately to the plight of the Serbian soldier (Captain Bluntschli), even though just a few moments earlier, she was delighting in Sergius' victory over the Serbs. And when there is the possibility of an actual slaughter taking place in her room (the Swiss soldier vowed to kill rather than be killed—even though we later discover that this was a bluff since he had no bullets), she impetuously decides to hide him and help him escape. When Bluntschli ridicules Sergius' quixotic cavalry charge, she *pretends* to be offended, but she is secretly glad that her intended is not "perfect."

Of Raina, Shaw wrote in an essay entitled "A Dramatic Realist to his Critics":

> The heroine [Raina] has been classified by critics as a minx, a liar, and a poseuse; I have nothing to do with that: the only moral question for me is, does she do good or harm? If you admit that she does good, that she generously saves a man's life and wisely extricates herself from a false position with another man, then you may classify her as you please—brave, generous and affectionate; or artful, dangerous, faithless—it is all one to me. . . .

Raina, then is perhaps a combination of all the above qualities. She is romantic, for example, when she remembers an opera (Verdi's *Ernani*) in which a member of the aristocracy shelters an enemy; thus, she shelters Bluntschli, since it is "chivalrous" to protect him. She does possess exalted ideals, but she is also pleased to step down from her pedestal and enjoy life directly; finally, in spite of her aristocratic background, she marries a person with "the soul of a hotel keeper."

Captain Bluntschli

Captain Bluntschli is a thirty-four-year-old realist who sees through the absurd romanticism of war. Furthermore, unlike the aristocratic volunteers who are untrained, amateurish idealists, Captain Bluntschli is a professional soldier, trained in waging a war in a highly efficient, businesslike manner. These methods allow Sergius to refer to his ability to wage a war as being low-class commercialism, devoid of any honor and nobility. Bluntschli would agree with this appraisal since he sees nothing romantic about the violent and senseless slaughter of human beings, even though it is his profession.

Being a professional soldier, he adopts a practical and wise view (his name is a combination of *Blunt*, plus the ending, which in Swiss means "sweet" or "endearing" or "lovable"). Given the choice of being killed or saving his life by climbing up a balcony and into a lady's bedroom, he chooses unheroically *not* to be killed. Practically, he knows that a dead professional soldier is of no value to anyone; thus, he saves his life by the most expedient method available—he hides in a lady's bedchamber. Likewise, given the choice of killing someone or of not going hungry, he chooses to eat rather than to kill; thus, he carries chocolates rather than cartridges, a highly unromantic but a very practical thing to do.

When Bluntschli first hears of Sergius' cavalry charge and refuses to view Sergius' actions in any way except as a foolhardy display of false heroics, he reveals his complete practicality and subjects himself to Raina's charge that he is "incapable of appreciating honor and courage." Yet, his questioning of Sergius' actions causes Raina to question Sergius' qualities.

Bluntschli does possess some qualities which cause Raina to exchange the "noble and heroic" Sergius in favor of him. Raina's perfect honesty, in fact, allows her to relax and to come down from her pedestal. Bluntschli's fondness for chocolates in the midst of war is appealingly incongruous. His docility, combined with his efficiency, endears him to others, especially the entire Petkoff family; and, finally, he reveals to the established group that he is an incurable romantic. He explains that he could have sent the old coat back, but that he wanted to return it personally so that he could have one more glimpse of the entrancing Raina. Thus, he wins her for his "affianced wife."

Sergius Saranoff

Sergius is the epitome of what every romantic hero should be: he is dashing, swashbuckling, devastatingly handsome, idealistic, wealthy, aristocratic, brave, and the acclaimed hero of a recent crushing victory in a recent cavalry raid which he led. He is possessed of only the loftiest and most noble ideals concerning war, romance, and chivalry, and he represents the quintessence of what a noble Bulgarian aristocrat should be. Yet, Sergius is more than this. He is an aristocrat, but he is a Byronic type who has certain ideals, and he is likely to become thoroughly disillusioned when these ideals fail. For example, Sergius did go to war filled with high ideals, and he did lead a heroic and courageous cavalry attack; later, however, he discovered that wars are not conducted by bravery and courage; they are more often waged and won better by efficient and practical planning than they are won by glorious and chivalric deeds. For Sergius, then, war is only fit for sons of hotel keepers, who have something of the tradesman about them. For that reason, Sergius has resigned from the army in complete disillusionment.

After having become cynical about soldiering, Sergius becomes skeptical about his relationship with Raina. After all, as he tells Louka, it is rather tiresome having to live up to Raina's "ideal of the higher love." It was he, however, who placed Raina on a pedestal so high, in fact, that he was blinded to any possible fault she might have. When Louka reveals all of Raina's faults—Raina lies, she pretends, and she has entertained another man in her bedroom—Sergius then feels free to cast his affections where they normally lead him—into marriage with the attractive Louka.

QUESTIONS FOR REVIEW

1. What is the source and irony of the title of this play?

2. While Shaw uses many elements of farce, this is still called a "drama of ideas." Discuss Shaw's use of farce to demonstrate some of his ideas.

3. What is meant by the subtitle "An Anti-Romantic Comedy"?

4. Which character best serves as Shaw's spokesman?

5. Shaw rejected romanticism and embraced realism. How realistic is *Arms and the Man*? How much of it is "unrealistic"?

6. How does Sergius' view of war differ from Bluntschli's?

7. Other than being used for his farcical actions, how does Nicola function in the drama?

8. Is Louka's entrapment of Sergius believable?

74

SELECTED BIBLIOGRAPHY

DUFFIN, H. C. *The Quintessence of Bernard Shaw.* London, 1920.

FULLER, EDMUND. *George Bernard Shaw, Critic of Western Morale.* New York, 1950.

HOWE, P. P. *Bernard Shaw.* London, 1915.

IRVINE, WILLIAM. *The Universe of GBS.* New York, 1949.

KRONENBERGER, LOUIS, ed. *George Bernard Shaw: A Critical Survey.* Cleveland and New York, 1953.

MENCKEN, H. L. *George Bernard Shaw: His Plays.* Boston, 1905.

RATTRAY, R. F. *Bernard Shaw: A Chronicle and an Introduction.* London, 1951.

SKIMPOLE, HERBERT. *Bernard Shaw: The Man and His Work.* London, 1918.

STRAUSS, E. *Bernard Shaw, Art, and Socialism.* London, 1942.

WARD, A. C. *Bernard Shaw.* London, 1951.

NOTES

NOTES

NOTES

NOTES

NOTES

NOTES